Contract Remedies

JANE M. FRIEDMAN

BLACK'S LAW DICTIONARY, FIFTH EDITION

One of the country's most used law books now completely revised to be more useful than ever

Black's Law Dictionary has been considered a standard —something "commonly used and accepted as an authority"* —for almost a century. Now, with the publication of the all new fifth edition of Black's, that definition is more applicable than ever.

We wouldn't have completely revised one of the country's most used law books unless we were sure we could make it even better. We have.

The new Black's brings you new terms, new guides, new features and new appendices. Among its more than 10,000 new entries are terms like "brain death," which reflect recent developments in the law. There are pronunciation guides in the main text of the book for the first time, and you'll find hundreds of references to federal court rules, Uniform Commercial Code, Internal Revenue Code and such recent legislation as the new Bankruptcy and Copyright Acts.

Black's Law Dictionary has been a basic requirement for sound law study for 88 years. Only a new Black's could hope to replace it as the standard for accurate, authoritative and comprehensive coverage of today's legal terms.

Act today to make this new standard yours.

*American Heritage Dictionary of the English Language, New College Edition

WEST PUBLISHING COMPANY
50 W. Kellogg Blvd., P.O. Box 64526 St. Paul, MN 55164

Also available in Deluxe leatherbound and Abridged softcover editions

Nutshell Series

of

WEST PUBLISHING COMPANY

P.O. Box 64526

St. Paul, Minnesota 55164-0526

Accounting—Law and, 1984, 377 pages, by E. McGruder Faris, Late Professor of Law, Stetson University.

Administrative Law and Process, 2nd Ed., 1981, 445 pages, by Ernest Gellhorn, Former Dean and Professor of Law, Case Western Reserve University and Barry B. Boyer, Professor of Law, SUNY, Buffalo.

Admiralty, 2nd Ed., 1988, about 362 pages, by Frank L. Maraist, Professor of Law, Louisiana State University.

Agency-Partnership, 1977, 364 pages, by Roscoe T. Steffen, Late Professor of Law, University of Chicago.

American Indian Law, 1981, 288 pages, by William C. Canby, Jr., Adjunct Professor of Law, Arizona State University.

Antitrust Law and Economics, 3rd Ed., 1986, 472 pages, by Ernest Gellhorn, Former Dean and Professor of Law, Case Western Reserve University.

Appellate Advocacy, 1984, 325 pages, by Alan D. Hornstein, Professor of Law, University of Maryland.

Art Law, 1984, 335 pages, by Leonard D. DuBoff, Professor of Law, Lewis and Clark College, Northwestern School of Law.

Banking and Financial Institutions, 1984, 409 pages, by William A. Lovett, Professor of Law, Tulane University.

Church-State Relations—Law of, 1981, 305 pages, by Leonard F. Manning, Late Professor of Law, Fordham University.

Civil Procedure, 2nd Ed., 1986, 306 pages, by Mary Kay Kane, Professor of Law, University of California, Hastings College of the Law.

Civil Rights, 1978, 279 pages, by Norman Vieira, Professor of Law, Southern Illinois University.

Commercial Paper, 3rd Ed., 1982, 404 pages, by Charles M. Weber, Professor of Business Law, University of Arizona and Richard E. Speidel, Professor of Law, Northwestern University.

Community Property, 2nd Ed., 1988, about 420 pages, by Robert L. Mennell, Former Professor of Law, Hamline University and Thomas M. Boykoff.

Comparative Legal Traditions, 1982, 402 pages, by Mary Ann Glendon, Professor of Law, Harvard University, Michael Wallace Gordon, Professor of Law, University of Florida and Christopher Osakwe, Professor of Law, Tulane University.

Conflicts, 1982, 470 pages, by David D. Siegel, Professor of Law, St. John's University.

Constitutional Analysis, 1979, 388 pages, by Jerre S. Williams, Professor of Law Emeritus, University of Texas.

Constitutional Federalism, 2nd Ed., 1987, 411 pages, by David E. Engdahl, Professor of Law, University of Puget Sound.

Constitutional Law, 1986, 389 pages, by Jerome A. Barron, Dean and Professor of Law, George Washington University and C. Thomas Dienes, Professor of Law, George Washington University.

Consumer Law, 2nd Ed., 1981, 418 pages, by David G. Epstein, Dean and Professor of Law, Emory University and Steve H. Nickles, Professor of Law, University of Minnesota.

Contract Remedies, 1981, 323 pages, by Jane M. Friedman, Professor of Law, Wayne State University.

Contracts, 2nd Ed., 1984, 425 pages, by Gordon D. Schaber, Dean and Professor of Law, McGeorge School of Law and Claude D. Rohwer, Professor of Law, McGeorge School of Law.

Corporations—Law of, 2nd Ed., 1987, 515 pages, by Robert W. Hamilton, Professor of Law, University of Texas.

Corrections and Prisoners' Rights—Law of, 2nd Ed., 1983, 386 pages, by Sheldon Krantz, Dean and Professor of Law, University of San Diego.

Criminal Law, 2nd Ed., 1987, 321 pages, by Arnold H. Loewy, Professor of Law, University of North Carolina.

Criminal Procedure—Constitutional Limitations, 4th Ed., 1988, about 461 pages, by Jerold H. Israel, Professor of Law, University of Michigan and Wayne R. LaFave, Professor of Law, University of Illinois.

Debtor-Creditor Law, 3rd Ed., 1986, 383 pages, by David G. Epstein, Dean and Professor of Law, Emory University.

Employment Discrimination—Federal Law of, 2nd Ed., 1981, 402 pages, by Mack A. Player, Professor of Law, University of Georgia.

Energy Law, 1981, 338 pages, by Joseph P. Tomain, Professor of Law, University of Cincinnatti.

Environmental Law, 1983, 343 pages by Roger W. Findley, Professor of Law, University of Illinois and Daniel A. Farber, Professor of Law, University of Minnesota.

Estate and Gift Taxation, Federal, 3rd Ed., 1983, 509 pages, by John K. McNulty, Professor of Law, University of California, Berkeley.

Estate Planning—Introduction to, 3rd Ed., 1983, 370 pages, by Robert J. Lynn, Professor of Law, Ohio State University.

Evidence, Federal Rules of, 2nd Ed., 1987, 473 pages, by Michael H. Graham, Professor of Law, University of Miami.

Evidence, State and Federal Rules, 2nd Ed., 1981, 514 pages, by Paul F. Rothstein, Professor of Law, Georgetown University.

Family Law, 2nd Ed., 1986, 444 pages, by Harry D. Krause, Professor of Law, University of Illinois.

Federal Jurisdiction, 2nd Ed., 1981, 258 pages, by David P. Currie, Professor of Law, University of Chicago.

Future Interests, 1981, 361 pages, by Lawrence W. Waggoner, Professor of Law, University of Michigan.

NUTSHELL SERIES

Government Contracts, 1979, 423 pages, by W. Noel Keyes, Professor of Law, Pepperdine University.

Historical Introduction to Anglo-American Law, 2nd Ed., 1973, 280 pages, by Frederick G. Kempin, Jr., Professor of Business Law, Wharton School of Finance and Commerce, University of Pennsylvania.

Immigration Law and Procedure, 1984, 345 pages, by David Weissbrodt, Professor of Law, University of Minnesota.

Injunctions, 1974, 264 pages, by John F. Dobbyn, Professor of Law, Villanova University.

Insurance Law, 1981, 281 pages, by John F. Dobbyn, Professor of Law, Villanova University.

Intellectual Property—Patents, Trademarks and Copyright, 1983, 428 pages, by Arthur R. Miller, Professor of Law, Harvard University, and Michael H. Davis, Professor of Law, Cleveland State University, Cleveland-Marshall College of Law.

International Business Transactions, 2nd Ed., 1984, 476 pages, by Donald T. Wilson, Late Professor of Law, Loyola University, Los Angeles.

International Law (Public), 1985, 262 pages, by Thomas Buergenthal, Professor of Law, Emory University and Harold G. Maier, Professor of Law, Vanderbilt University.

Introduction to the Study and Practice of Law, 1983, 418 pages, by Kenney F. Hegland, Professor of Law, University of Arizona.

Judicial Process, 1980, 292 pages, by William L. Reynolds, Professor of Law, University of Maryland.

Jurisdiction, 4th Ed., 1980, 232 pages, by Albert A. Ehrenzweig, Late Professor of Law, University of California, Berkeley, David W. Louisell, Late Professor of Law, University of California, Berkeley and Geoffrey C. Hazard, Jr., Professor of Law, Yale Law School.

Juvenile Courts, 3rd Ed., 1984, 291 pages, by Sanford J. Fox, Professor of Law, Boston College.

Labor Arbitration Law and Practice, 1979, 358 pages, by Dennis R. Nolan, Professor of Law, University of South Carolina.

Labor Law, 2nd Ed., 1986, 397 pages, by Douglas L. Leslie, Professor of Law, University of Virginia.

Land Use, 2nd Ed., 1985, 356 pages, by Robert R. Wright, Professor of Law, University of Arkansas, Little Rock and Susan Webber Wright, Professor of Law, University of Arkansas, Little Rock.

Landlord and Tenant Law, 2nd Ed., 1986, 311 pages, by David S. Hill, Professor of Law, University of Colorado.

Law Study and Law Examinations—Introduction to, 1971, 389 pages, by Stanley V. Kinyon, Late Professor of Law, University of Minnesota.

Legal Interviewing and Counseling, 2nd Ed., 1987, 487 pages, by Thomas L. Shaffer, Professor of Law, Washington and Lee University and James R. Elkins, Professor of Law, West Virginia University.

Legal Research, 4th Ed., 1985, 452 pages, by Morris L. Cohen, Professor of Law and Law Librarian, Yale University.

Legal Writing, 1982, 294 pages, by Lynn B. Squires and Marjorie Dick Rombauer, Professor of Law, University of Washington.

Legislative Law and Process, 2nd Ed., 1986, 346 pages, by Jack Davies, Professor of Law, William Mitchell College of Law.

Local Government Law, 2nd Ed., 1983, 404 pages, by David J. McCarthy, Jr., Professor of Law, Georgetown University.

Mass Communications Law, 3rd Ed., 1988, 538 pages, by Harvey L. Zuckman, Professor of Law, Catholic University, Martin J. Gaynes, Lecturer in Law, Temple University, T. Barton Carter, Professor of Public Communications, Boston University, and Juliet Lushbough Dee, Professor of Communications, University of Delaware.

Medical Malpractice—The Law of, 2nd Ed., 1986, 342 pages, by Joseph H. King, Professor of Law, University of Tennessee.

NUTSHELL SERIES

Military Law, 1980, 378 pages, by Charles A. Shanor, Professor of Law, Emory University and Timothy P. Terrell, Professor of Law, Emory University.

Oil and Gas Law, 1983, 443 pages, by John S. Lowe, Professor of Law, Southern Methodist University.

Personal Property, 1983, 322 pages, by Barlow Burke, Jr., Professor of Law, American University.

Post-Conviction Remedies, 1978, 360 pages, by Robert Popper, Dean and Professor of Law, University of Missouri, Kansas City.

Presidential Power, 1977, 328 pages, by Arthur Selwyn Miller, Professor of Law Emeritus, George Washington University.

Products Liability, 3rd Ed., 1988, about 350 pages, by Jerry J. Phillips, Professor of Law, University of Tennessee.

Professional Responsibility, 1980, 399 pages, by Robert H. Aronson, Professor of Law, University of Washington, and Donald T. Weckstein, Professor of Law, University of San Diego.

Real Estate Finance, 2nd Ed., 1985, 262 pages, by Jon W. Bruce, Professor of Law, Vanderbilt University.

Real Property, 2nd Ed., 1981, 448 pages, by Roger H. Bernhardt, Professor of Law, Golden Gate University.

Regulated Industries, 2nd Ed., 1987, 389 pages, by Ernest Gellhorn, Former Dean and Professor of Law, Case Western Reserve University, and Richard J. Pierce, Professor of Law, Southern Methodist University.

Remedies, 2nd Ed., 1985, 320 pages, by John F. O'Connell, Dean and Professor of Law, Southern California College of Law.

Res Judicata, 1976, 310 pages, by Robert C. Casad, Professor of Law, University of Kansas.

Sales, 2nd Ed., 1981, 370 pages, by John M. Stockton, Professor of Business Law, Wharton School of Finance and Commerce, University of Pennsylvania.

Schools, Students and Teachers—Law of, 1984, 409 pages, by Kern Alexander, President, Western Kentucky University and M. David Alexander, Professor, Virginia Tech University.

Sea—Law of, 1984, 264 pages, by Louis B. Sohn, Professor of Law, University of Georgia and Kristen Gustafson.

Secured Transactions, 2nd Ed., 1981, 391 pages, by Henry J. Bailey, Professor of Law Emeritus, Willamette University.

Securities Regulation, 3rd Ed., 1988, about 350 pages, by David L. Ratner, Dean and Professor of Law, University of San Francisco.

Sex Discrimination, 1982, 399 pages, by Claire Sherman Thomas, Lecturer, University of Washington, Women's Studies Department.

Taxation and Finance, State and Local, 1986, 309 pages, by M. David Gelfand, Professor of Law, Tulane University and Peter W. Salsich, Professor of Law, St. Louis University.

Taxation of Individuals, Federal Income, 3rd Ed., 1983, 487 pages, by John K. McNulty, Professor of Law, University of California, Berkeley.

Torts—Injuries to Persons and Property, 1977, 434 pages, by Edward J. Kionka, Professor of Law, Southern Illinois University.

Torts—Injuries to Family, Social and Trade Relations, 1979, 358 pages, by Wex S. Malone, Professor of Law Emeritus, Louisiana State University.

Trial Advocacy, 1979, 402 pages, by Paul B. Bergman, Adjunct Professor of Law, University of California, Los Angeles.

Trial and Practice Skills, 1978, 346 pages, by Kenney F. Hegland, Professor of Law, University of Arizona.

Trial, The First—Where Do I Sit? What Do I Say?, 1982, 396 pages, by Steven H. Goldberg, Professor of Law, University of Minnesota.

Unfair Trade Practices, 1982, 445 pages, by Charles R. McManis, Professor of Law, Washington University.

Uniform Commercial Code, 2nd Ed., 1984, 516 pages, by Bradford Stone, Professor of Law, Stetson University.

Uniform Probate Code, 2nd Ed., 1987, 454 pages, by Lawrence H. Averill, Jr., Dean and Professor of Law, University of Arkansas, Little Rock.

Hornbook Series

and

Basic Legal Texts

of

WEST PUBLISHING COMPANY

P.O. Box 64526

St. Paul, Minnesota 55164–0526

Admiralty and Maritime Law, Schoenbaum's Hornbook on, 1987, 692 pages, by Thomas J. Schoenbaum, Professor of Law, University of Georgia.

Agency and Partnership, Reuschlein & Gregory's Hornbook on the Law of, 1979 with 1981 Pocket Part, 625 pages, by Harold Gill Reuschlein, Professor of Law Emeritus, Villanova University and William A. Gregory, Professor of Law, Georgia State University.

Antitrust, Sullivan's Hornbook on the Law of, 1977, 886 pages, by Lawrence A. Sullivan, Professor of Law, University of California, Berkeley.

Civil Procedure, Friedenthal, Kane and Miller's Hornbook on, 1985, 876 pages, by Jack H. Friedental, Professor of Law, Stanford University, Mary Kay Kane, Professor of Law, University of California, Hastings College of the Law and Arthur R. Miller, Professor of Law, Harvard University.

Common Law Pleading, Koffler and Reppy's Hornbook on, 1969, 663 pages, by Joseph H. Koffler, Professor of Law, New York Law School and Alison Reppy, Late Dean and Professor of Law, New York Law School.

Conflict of Laws, Scoles and Hay's Hornbook on, 1982, with 1986 Pocket Part, 1085 pages, by Eugene F. Scoles, Professor of Law, University of Illinois and Peter Hay, Dean and Professor of Law, University of Illinois.

Constitutional Law, Nowak, Rotunda and Young's Hornbook on, 3rd Ed., 1986, 1191 pages, by John E. Nowak, Professor of Law, University of Illinois, Ronald D. Rotunda, Professor of Law, University of Illinois, and J. Nelson Young, Late Professor of Law, University of North Carolina.

Contracts, Calamari and Perillo's Hornbook on, 3rd Ed., 1987, 1049 pages, by John D. Calamari, Professor of Law, Fordham University and Joseph M. Perillo, Professor of Law, Fordham University.

Contracts, Corbin's One Volume Student Ed., 1952, 1224 pages, by Arthur L. Corbin, Late Professor of Law, Yale University.

Corporations, Henn and Alexander's Hornbook on, 3rd Ed., 1983, with 1986 Pocket Part, 1371 pages, by Harry G. Henn, Professor of Law Emeritus, Cornell University and John R. Alexander.

Criminal Law, LaFave and Scott's Hornbook on, 2nd Ed., 1986, 918 pages, by Wayne R. LaFave, Professor of Law, University of Illinois, and Austin Scott, Jr., Late Professor of Law, University of Colorado.

Criminal Procedure, LaFave and Israel's Hornbook on, 1985 with 1986 pocket part, 1142 pages, by Wayne R. LaFave, Professor of Law, University of Illinois and Jerold H. Israel, Professor of Law University of Michigan.

Damages, McCormick's Hornbook on, 1935, 811 pages, by Charles T. McCormick, Late Dean and Professor of Law, University of Texas.

Domestic Relations, Clark's Hornbook on, 2nd Ed., 1988, about 1100 pages, by Homer H. Clark, Jr., Professor of Law, University of Colorado.

Economics and Federal Antitrust Law, Hovenkamp's Hornbook on, 1985, 414 pages, by Herbert Hovenkamp, Professor of Law, University of Iowa.

Employment Discrimination Law, Player's Hornbook on, about 650 pages, 1988, by Mack A. Player, Professor of Law, University of Georgia.

Environmental Law, Rodgers' Hornbook on, 1977 with 1984 Pocket Part, 956 pages, by William H. Rodgers, Jr., Professor of Law, University of Washington.

Evidence, Lilly's Introduction to, 2nd Ed., 1987, 585 pages, by Graham C. Lilly, Professor of Law, University of Virginia.

Evidence, McCormick's Hornbook on, 3rd Ed., 1984 with 1987 Pocket Part, 1156 pages, General Editor, Edward W. Cleary, Professor of Law Emeritus, Arizona State University.

Federal Courts, Wright's Hornbook on, 4th Ed., 1983, 870 pages, by Charles Alan Wright, Professor of Law, University of Texas.

Federal Income Taxation, Rose and Chommie's Hornbook on, 3rd Ed., 1988, about 875 pages, by Michael D. Rose, Professor of Law, Ohio State University and John C. Chommie, Late Professor of Law, University of Miami.

Federal Income Taxation of Individuals, Posin's Hornbook on, 1983 with 1987 Pocket Part, 491 pages, by Daniel Q. Posin, Jr., Professor of Law, Catholic University.

Future Interest, Simes' Hornbook on, 2nd Ed., 1966, 355 pages, by Lewis M. Simes, Late Professor of Law, University of Michigan.

Insurance, Keeton and Widiss' Basic Text on, 1988, about 1000 pages, by Robert E. Keeton, Professor of Law Emeritus, Harvard University and Alan I. Widiss, Professor of Law, University of Iowa.

Labor Law, Gorman's Basic Text on, 1976, 914 pages, by Robert A. Gorman, Professor of Law, University of Pennsylvania.

Law Problems, Ballentine's, 5th Ed., 1975, 767 pages, General Editor, William E. Burby, Late Professor of Law, University of Southern California.

Legal Ethics, Wolfram's Hornbook on, 1986, 1120 pages, by Charles W. Wolfram, Professor of Law, Cornell University.

Legal Writing Style, Weihofen's, 2nd Ed., 1980, 332 pages, by Henry Weihofen, Professor of Law Emeritus, University of New Mexico.

Local Government Law, Reynolds' Hornbook on, 1982 with 1987 Pocket Part, 860 pages, by Osborne M. Reynolds, Professor of Law, University of Oklahoma.

New York Estate Administration, Turano and Radigan's Hornbook on, 1986, 676 pages, by Margaret V. Turano, Professor of Law, St. John's University and Raymond Radigan.

New York Practice, Siegel's Hornbook on, 1978 with 1987 Pocket Part, 1011 pages, by David D. Siegel, Professor of Law, St. John's University.

Oil and Gas Law, Hemingway's Hornbook on, 2nd Ed., 1983, with 1986 Pocket Part, 543 pages, by Richard W. Hemingway, Professor of Law, University of Oklahoma.

Property, Boyer's Survey of, 3rd Ed., 1981, 766 pages, by Ralph E. Boyer, Professor of Law Emeritus, University of Miami.

Property, Law of, Cunningham, Whitman and Stoebuck's Hornbook on, 1984, with 1987 Pocket Part, 916 pages, by Roger A. Cunningham, Professor of Law, University of Michigan, Dale A. Whitman, Dean and Professor of Law, University of Missouri, Columbia and William B. Stoebuck, Professor of Law, University of Washington.

Real Estate Finance Law, Nelson and Whitman's Hornbook on, 2nd Ed., 1985, 941 pages, by Grant S. Nelson, Professor of Law, University of Missouri, Columbia and Dale A. Whitman, Dean and Professor of Law, University of Missouri, Columbia.

Real Property, Moynihan's Introduction to, 2nd Ed., 1987, 239 pages, by Cornelius J. Moynihan, Late Professor of Law, Suffolk University.

Remedies, Dobbs' Hornbook on, 1973, 1067 pages, by Dan B. Dobbs, Professor of Law, University of Arizona.

Secured Transactions under the U.C.C., Henson's Hornbook on, 2nd Ed., 1979 with 1979 Pocket Part, 504 pages, by Ray D. Henson, Professor of Law, University of California, Hastings College of the Law.

Securities Regulation, Hazen's Hornbook on the Law of, 1985, with 1988 Pocket Part, 739 pages, by Thomas Lee Hazen, Professor of Law, University of North Carolina.

Sports Law, Schubert, Smith and Trentadue's, 1986, 395 pages, by George W. Schubert, Dean of University College, University of North Dakota, Rodney K. Smith, Professor of Law, Delaware Law School, Widener University, and Jesse C. Trentadue, Former Professor of Law, University of North Dakota.

Torts, Prosser and Keeton's Hornbook on, 5th Ed., 1984 with 1988 Pocket Part, 1286 pages, by William L. Prosser, Late Dean and Professor of Law, University of California, Berkeley, Page Keeton, Professor of Law Emeritus, University of Texas, Dan B. Dobbs, Professor of Law, University of Arizona, Robert E. Keeton, Professor of Law Emeritus, Harvard University and David G. Owen, Professor of Law, University of South Carolina.

Trial Advocacy, Jeans' Handbook on, Soft cover, 1975, 473 pages, by James W. Jeans, Professor of Law, University of Missouri, Kansas City.

Trusts, Bogert's Hornbook on, 6th Ed., 1987, 794 pages, by George T. Bogert.

Uniform Commercial Code, White and Summers' Hornbook on, 3rd Ed., 1988, about 1250 pages, by James J. White, Professor of Law, University of Michigan and Robert S. Summers, Professor of Law, Cornell University.

Urban Planning and Land Development Control Law, Hagman and Juergensmeyer's Hornbook on, 2nd Ed., 1986, 680 pages, by Donald G. Hagman, Late Professor of Law, University of California, Los Angeles and Julian C. Juergensmeyer, Professor of Law, University of Florida.

Wills, Atkinson's Hornbook on, 2nd Ed., 1953, 975 pages, by Thomas E. Atkinson, Late Professor of Law, New York University.

Wills, Trusts and Estates, McGovern, Rein and Kurtz' Hornbook on, 1988, by William M. McGovern, Professor of Law, University of California, Los Angeles, Jan Ellen Rein, Professor of Law, Gonzaga University, and Sheldon F. Kurtz, Professor of Law, University of Iowa.

Advisory Board

CONTRACT REMEDIES
IN A NUTSHELL

By

JANE M. FRIEDMAN
Professor of Law
Wayne State University

ST. PAUL, MINN.
WEST PUBLISHING CO.
1981

Library of Congress Cataloging in Publication Data

Friedman, Jane M.
    Contract remedies in a nutshell.

    (Nutshell series)
    Includes index.
    1. Breach of contract—United States. 2. Equitable
remedies—United States. I. Title.
II. Series.
KF836.Z9F75   346.73'022   81–11614
                   347.30622   AACR2

    0–314–60373–5

    Friedman Contract Remedies
    2nd Reprint—1988

This book is dedicated
to the memory of Harry, Pearl, and
Edward Goldbarg

The author wishes to express her gratitude for the assistance of Leonard Crowley, Lynn Klobuchar, and Rina Wallack

SUMMARY OF CONTENTS

SUMMARY OF CONTENTS

PART III. CONTRACTUAL CONTROL OVER REMEDY

PART IV. REMEDIES FOR MISTAKE AND UNCONSCIONABILITY

OUTLINE

Chapter 7. Remedies Available to Seller When Buyer Defaults and Has Note Accepted the Goods—Cont'd

OUTLINE

OUTLINE

TABLE OF REFERENCES TO UNIFORM COMMERCIAL CODE AND OFFICIAL COMMENTS

References are to Pages

TABLE OF REFERENCES

TABLE OF REFERENCES

TABLE OF REFERENCES

TABLE OF REFERENCES

*

CONTRACT REMEDIES
in a
Nutshell

PART I

COMMON LAW AND EQUITABLE REMEDIES FOR BREACH OF CONTRACT

INTRODUCTION

The purpose of Part I is to describe and analyze the common law and equitable remedies available to a party who has been aggrieved by a breach of contract. With a few exceptions (which will be noted as they occur) Part I will be based on four assumptions: (1) that a valid contract exists between plaintiff and defendant, (2) that defendant has breached the contract, (3) that defendant has no defenses which can be successfully asserted against plaintiff's claim for breach, and (4) that the contract itself does not provide for a remedy or limitation on remedy. The question which then arises is: what remedies are available to the aggrieved plaintiff? Several options are available; they are summarized below, and then discussed in detail in Chapters One through Four.

[1]

Expectation Damages

When a contract has been breached, the primary function of the law of damages is to place the injured party in as good a position as he would have been in had the contract been fully performed. Damages which are awarded for this purpose are called either "expectation" or "loss of bargain" damages because they are an attempt to give the aggrieved plaintiff the full value of his bargain, i. e., the net gain he would have enjoyed had the contract not been breached. The vast majority of contract actions involve a claim for expectation damages, which is the topic explored in Chapter 1.

Restitution and Reliance Damages

Protection of the expectation interest is clearly the primary concern of the law of contract damages. That law, however, also has two secondary concerns—protection of the restitution interest and compensation for injury to the reliance interest. The restitution interest represents plaintiffs interest in recouping the benefits which he conferred on defendant prior to defendant's breach. In contrast, the reliance interest represents the detriment that plaintiff has incurred by changing his position in reliance on his belief that defendant would fulfill his part of the bargain. An award of restitution (the subject of Chapter 2) or, alternatively, of reliance damages (the subject of

[2]

Chapter 3) usually serves the function of returning plaintiff to the status quo ante—the position which he occupied before entering into the contract.

Specific Performance

There are occasions when an award of money damages (based either on the expectation interest, the restitution interest, or the reliance interest) will be inadequate to provide full and complete compensation to the injured plaintiff. In such cases, the courts have discretion to enter a decree of specific performance—an order which compels the breaching party to actually render the performance agreed upon instead of providing compensation in "mere" money. Specific performance (the subject of Chapter 4) is a form of equitable relief and will not be available unless the plaintiff can demonstrate that money damages will not adequately compensate him for his injury.

CHAPTER 1

EXPECTATION DAMAGES

When a contract has been breached, the primary function of the law of damages is to place the injured party in as good a position as he would have been in had the contract been fully performed. Damages which are awarded for this purpose are called either "expectation" or "loss of bargain" damages because they are an attempt to give the aggrieved plaintiff the full value of his bargain, i. e., the net gain he would have enjoyed had the contract not been breached. Thus, expectation damages are a somewhat unique remedy in that they "compensate" the injured party for something he never had in the first place.

§ 1.1 Measuring the "Loss of Bargain" or "Expectation"

A breach of contract usually causes the aggrieved party to be "injured" in the sense that he is prevented from attaining something that full performance of the contract would have given him. In addition, a breach will sometimes cause plaintiff's position to be worse than it was prior to contracting by virtue of depriving him of something which he previously enjoyed. In order to determine the amount of damages necessary to compensate the plaintiff for his loss of bargain, it

[4]

is necessary to consider both of these types of injury. Expectation damages will be given for the value of the *gains prevented* by the breach (expected additions to plaintiff's wealth) and *losses suffered* thereby (actual subtractions from plaintiff's pre-existing wealth). However, from this amount must be subtracted the *costs* which plaintiff has *avoided* (usually because of plaintiff's being excused from rendering the balance of his own performance) and any *gains made possible* by virtue of defendant's breach.

(a) Formula

Loss of bargain = value of gains prevented + amount of losses suffered (other than "reliance losses") (See Chapter 3) − costs avoided − gains made possible.

EXAMPLE 1. Builder X contracts with owner Y to construct a building on Y's land for $50,000, payable on completion. Y breaches by repudiating the contract soon after its making. At the time of breach, X has not incurred any expenses in performance or preparation for performance. It would have cost X $40,000 to construct the building. X sues Y for damages. X's loss of bargain equals the value of gains prevented ($50,000) + amount of other losses suffered (0) − costs avoided ($40,000) − gains made possible (0), or $10,000.

EXAMPLE 2. Builder X contracts with owner Y to construct an annex to a building already owned by Y. The contract price is $20,000 payable upon completion. X begins construction of the annex but because of the use of substandard materials, the structure falls to the ground and is rendered totally worthless except for scrap. X refuses to attempt re-construction, and Y is unable to find another builder to do the work. Y sells the scrap materials for a reasonable price, $3,000, and subsequently sues for breach of contract. At trial, she is able to prove that (1) had X fully performed, the completed annex would have enhanced the market value of Y's property in the amount of $30,000. (2) When the annex collapsed, it fell against the adjacent building (owned by Y), damaging that building in the amount of $8,000. Y's loss of bargain equals the value of gains prevented ($30,000) + amount of other losses suffered ($8,000) − costs avoided ($20,000) − gains made possible ($3,000), or $15,000.

(b) What Is Meant by "Value"

In the formula set forth above, the part of the equation which gives rise to the most difficulty is "value of gains prevented". This is because the concept of "value" is variable and dependent on the type of performance which has been promised.

When the promised performance involves only the payment of money, valuation usually poses no problem. Subject to the rules regarding "mitigation of damages" (§ 1.2 infra) and special formulae for sales of goods contracts (Chapters 5 through 8 infra) the value of a broken promise to pay money is simply the unpaid amount of money which defendant has agreed to pay.

When the promised performance involves something other than the payment of money (e. g. the delivery of goods or services) "value" is generally determined by the amount of money that plaintiff would have to pay to *another person* (real or hypothetical) to obtain an identical performance.

Market Value as Usual Standard

In determining what plaintiff would have to pay to "another person" to obtain an identical performance, market prices, when they exist, are usually determinative.

EXAMPLE. X and Y contract for the sale to Y by X of 100 shares of Lucky Jack Uranium stock for $1,000, payable on delivery. X repudiates the contract and refuses to deliver the stock. At the time Y learns of the breach, the market price for 100 shares of Lucky Jack stock is $1,400. The "value of gains prevented" is $1,400. Therefore, Y's "loss of bargain" is $1,400 minus costs avoided ($1,000) or $400.

Determining Value When There Is No Market

The "market value" standard can be easily applied in those cases where the promised performance involves goods or securities which are bought and sold at commodity and stock exchanges or some other type of established market. The standard obviously cannot be readily applied to other types of promised performances, such as the tender of a unique chattel or the rendering of professional services. In such cases, "value" is still determined by ascertaining what plaintiff would have to pay to another person (real or hypothetical) to obtain an identical performance. In the absence of a true market, however, valuation often becomes an uncertain process. In such cases, the courts require only a "reasonably certain" estimate of value.

Valuation of Realty or Unique Chattels: Evidence Deemed Admissible

In arriving at a determination of the value of realty or a unique chattel, the courts will generally admit the opinions of qualified experts as well as evidence of the sale price of the same realty or chattel if it was sold to someone other than plaintiff soon after breach. Some courts will also admit evidence of the sale price of *similar* realty or chattels in unrelated transactions, but only if the other property is substantially similar to the property at issue. In general, the courts will not hear evidence relating to the particular subjective value that the property may have had to plaintiff.

EXAMPLE 1. On January 2, Vendor and Vendee enter into a contract for the sale of Lot #2 on the 2100 block of Maple Street for $20,000. Title is to pass on April 30. On April 29, Vendor repudiates the contract and sells the land to X for $28,000. Vendee sues for damages. At trial, Vendee offers evidence of (1) the sale of Lot #2 to X for $28,000; (2) two sales by other vendors of lots on the 2100 block of Maple Street during the last few days of April. Plaintiff introduces official records showing that one of those lots was sold for $27,000 and the other for $30,000. All courts would admit evidence of the sale price of Lot #2. In addition, some courts would admit evidence of the sale price of the other two lots, as long as they are substantially similar to Lot #2 in size, location, and other characteristics.

EXAMPLE 2. Sister and Brother enter into a contract for the sale by Sister to Brother of a sterling silver samovar, a family heirloom, for $3,000. Sister repudiates the contract and sells the samovar to Cousin for $5,000. Brother sues for damages and at trial attempts to produce evidence of (1) the sale to Cousin for $5,000; (2) the opinion of a well-known antique dealer that the samovar would be worth $6,000 in the antique market; (3) the fact that the samovar has great sentimental value to Brother who recalls drinking Kool-Aid from it when he was a toddler. The courts would admit evidence of the sale to Cousin and the opinion of the expert. Evidence of the sentimental value of the property to plaintiff, however, would not be admissible.

[*9*]

Valuation of Personal Services: Evidence Deemed Admissible

If the promised performance involves personal services of a standardized nature, and there is in fact a "going rate" for such services, it will not be difficult to arrive at an estimate of their value. Indeed, the "going rate" for such services is in fact their "market value"; and loss of bargain can be determined in the same manner as for goods and securities for which there is an established market. However, when the promised performance is for the rendering of services for which there are great variations in skill, competency, judgment, etc., then there is not a general market value for these services because they derive their value from the fact that they were to be rendered by defendant.

EXAMPLE 1. Under the terms of a contract between X and Y, X is to hang wallpaper in seven rooms in Y's house for $500. X repudiates the contract, and Y sues. At trial, Y offers evidence of the fact that immediately after X's breach, Y approached three other wallpaper hangers about the job, and all quoted a price of $800. Assuming that wallpaper hanging is a standardized service, and one in which there are not great disparities in skill, competency, etc., evidence of the $800 figure is admissible to show the value of the performance promised by defendant.

EXAMPLE 2. Vladimir, a world-famous pianist, enters into a contract with his friend Natasha, whereby Vladimir agrees to give piano lessons to Natasha twice a week for one year for a price of $20 per hourly lesson. Vladimir repudiates the agreement, and Natasha sues. Vladimir attempts to introduce evidence that the "going rate" for lessons by experienced piano teachers is between $15 and $20 per hour. Consequently, he argues, Natasha has not been damaged by his breach. This evidence will probably be deemed inadmissible. The promised performance derives its value from the fact that the services were to be rendered by Vladimir. Suppose, however, that Natasha has evidence of the fact that at the time of breach, Vladimir was charging $50 per hour to all his other students. This evidence will be admissible for purposes of estimating the value of Vladimir's service.

(c) When the Cost of Performance Exceeds Its Objective Value

As has been previously discussed, the basic principle governing the award of expectation damages is that the aggrieved party is to be placed in as good a position as he would have been in had the contract not been breached. In one frequently occuring context, however, it is not clear what is meant by the phrase "in as good a position as he would have been". The problem arises, usually in the context of construction contracts, whenever the objective *value* to plaintiff of securing full per-

formance is less than what it would *cost* plaintiff
to obtain a similar performance from another person. Are plaintiff's expectation damages to be
measured by the *value* of the promised performance even though such an award will not compensate him for the *cost* of obtaining that performance from someone else? In general, the rule
is that damages are to be measured by the *cost* of
completing performance unless that cost is vastly
disproportionate to the value to be derived therefrom. When the cost does greatly exceed the value, many of the principles and policies which underlie the entire law of contract damages are
brought into conflict. In such cases, there are no
black-letter rules. Instead, the courts choose between the "cost of performance" measure and the
"diminished value" measure only after balancing
the policies and equities weighing in favor of and
against each of the parties.

Factors Favoring "Diminished Value" Instead of "Cost of Performance": Economic Waste and Unjust Enrichment

The term "diminished value" refers to the
amount by which the objective value of the contract has been reduced by virtue of defendant's
breach. It is simply the difference between the
value of what defendant promised to perform and
the value of what he actually did perform. In cases
where this "diminished value" is a much lesser

amount than it will cost plaintiff to obtain complete performance of the contract, two policies militating in favor of awarding the "diminished value" are the policy against economic waste and the policy against unjust enrichment.

Economic waste occurs whenever there is *unreasonable* destruction of completed work and/or usable property. (See immediately following example).

The term "unjust enrichment", used in the present context, means that if plaintiff were to recover any sum in excess of the *value* of the promised performance, he would probably pocket the recovery rather than use it to secure a similar performance from another person. The result would be that the "aggrieved" party would be left with a sum of money in excess of any objective harm done to him. Unjust enrichment and economic waste are often present at the same time. That is, if defendant's "defective" performance has left plaintiff with property which is usable in its present state (the destruction of which might result in "economic waste"), it is unlikely that plaintiff will actually use the damages awarded to remedy the defect. His failure to do so will mean that, to some extent, he will be unjustly enriched.

EXAMPLE. Under the terms of a contract between builder and owner, builder is to install plumbing with Brand X pipes in the house which he is constructing for owner. Due to an oversight, builder installs Brand Y pipes instead of Brand X. By the time this error is discovered, the plumbing is already encased within the walls. Substitution of Brand X would entail demolition and re-construction of substantial parts of the completed structure at a cost to builder of $20,000. The difference in value between a house with Brand X pipes and one with Brand Y is $50. Upon builder's refusal to tear down the structure in order to substitute Brand X for Brand Y, owner sues for breach. The complaint demands damages of $20,000 which represents the cost of securing the promised performance from another person. In such a case, the courts would probably use "diminished value" rather than "cost of performance" as the appropriate measure, resulting in an award of $50. To award the $20,000 would be to encourage economic waste in that it would induce future builders in similar cases to demolish and reconstruct completed work which is very usable in its present state, and which is substantially in compliance with the contract. Moreover, if the court were to award the "cost of performance" figure ($20,000), it is very unlikely that owner would use the money to tear apart the structure and substitute Brand X pipes. Thus, owner would be unjustly enriched because he would be left with a home substantially as valuable, usable, and livable as the one he contracted for, and a sum of money far in excess of any financial injury done to him.

[*14*]

Factors Favoring "Cost Of Performance" Instead of "Diminished Value": Frustration of Purpose and Inducement of Breach

Two other policy considerations often result in an award of the "cost to complete performance" figure. First, in some instances, unless plaintiff is awarded the entire "cost" figure, his contractual purpose may be frustrated. Second, an award of the lesser "diminished value" figure might induce future breaches of contract by defendant and/or others similarly situated.

Frustration of Purpose

Frustration of purpose occurs whenever the defect in performance renders the subject matter unusable for the purposes contemplated by plaintiff. This can happen either because the performance does not meet particular specifications which are necessary for plaintiff's purposes, or because plaintiff's purpose in contracting was to gratify some personal taste or whim. In such cases, in order for plaintiff to be put in "as good a position as he would have been in" had defendant not breached the contract, plaintiff should be awarded the *cost* of remedying the defect in performance.

EXAMPLE 1. Owner and builder enter into a contract for the construction of a home and attached garage with an access driveway. At the time of contracting, owner gives builder detailed specifications for the garage and driveway and insists that they be wide enough to accommodate owner's pickup truck, as this is his usual means of transportation. When construction is completed, it is discovered that builder has deviated from owner's specifications. Consequently, the driveway, although suitable for an automobile, is too narrow to be used safely and conveniently when driving a pickup truck. Builder refuses to remedy the defect, and owner sues. At trial, builder points out that there is no difference between the market value of the house as built and one with a wider driveway. He also proves that it would cost $5,000 to tear up the driveway and substitute a wider one. He argues that this would be wasteful and that owner is therefore entitled to damages representing the diminished value of the property, which, in this case, would result in an award of only nominal damages. (See subsection (g) infra for a discussion of nominal damages). Owner would probably be awarded the cost of curing the defect, or $5,000. An award of the "diminished value" would frustrate owner's purpose of providing shelter (and access thereto) for his pickup truck. Moreover, in the instant case, awarding the "cost of completing performance" will not violate the policy against unjust enrichment. It is likely that owner will undertake to remedy the defect by tearing up the driveway and constructing a wider one. Even if he does not, his loss of bargain is certainly more than nominal. Also, there is no *unreasonable* economic waste in this situation since the driveway is unusable (for the purposes contemplated by plaintiff) in its present condition.

EXAMPLE 2. X contracts to construct a marble statue of General Custer in Y's front yard for $3,000, but abandons the work after the foundation has been laid and before receiving any payment from Y. Y sues. At trial, X introduces unrebutted evidence that the contemplated statue is so aesthetically unappealing that it would actually *decrease* the market value of Y's property. Due to a rise in the price of labor and materials, it will now cost Y $5,000 to get another contractor to complete construction of the statue. Y can get a judgment based on the cost of completion. The courts have noted that a person "may do what he will with his own. . . . and if he chooses to erect a monument to his caprice or folly on his premises, and employs. . . . another to do it, it does not lie with a defendant who has been so employed. . . . to say that his own performance would not be beneficial to plaintiff." Of course, from the "cost of completion" figure ($5,000) must be deducted the cost which plaintiff has avoided by being excused from tendering the balance of his own performance ($3,000).

Inducement of Breach

The final, but by no means least important, policy consideration is that whenever a court awards the "diminished value" figure rather than the larger "cost to complete performance" measure, the effect of such a decision is to induce, rather than discourage, future breaches of contract by defendant and/or others similarly situated. For, if one who is contemplating breach knows that his liability will be for a lesser amount than it will cost him to complete performance, he will have a financial incentive to break his contract. But, of course, one of the aims of the law of contract damages is to discourage, rather than induce, breach. Therefore, in each case where one is faced with the issue of "cost of performance" versus "diminished value" as the appropriate measure of damages, one must consider whether the facts are such that it is important that the court not offer a financial inducement to future persons, similarly situated, to breach their agreements.

EXAMPLE 1. Under the terms of a contract between builder and owner, builder is to install plumbing with Brand X pipes in the house which he is constructing for owner. Due to an oversight, builder installs Brand Y pipes instead of Brand X. By the time the error is discovered, the plumbing is already encased within the walls. Substitution of Brand X would entail demolition and reconstruction of substantial parts of the completed structure at a cost to builder of $20,000. The difference in the market value between a house with Brand X pipes and one with Brand Y is $50. Upon builder's refusal to tear down the structure in order to substitute Brand X for Brand Y, owner sues for $20,000 in damages. As has been previously discussed, it is unlikely that owner will be able to recover $20,000 as such an award would result in economic waste and unjust enrichment. In addition, many courts would consider whether the facts are such that it is important that future builders, when faced with a similar problem, be induced to remedy the defect. Such facts are not present in this example, particularly since builder appears to be in substantial compliance with the contract, and his breach was not intentional. Thus, the "diminished value", $50, is the appropriate measure of recovery.

EXAMPLE 2. X, who owns a farm containing coal deposits, leases the premises to Y for a period of five years for coal mining purposes. A "strip mining" operation is contemplated in which coal will be taken from pits on the surface of the ground. In addition to other agreements contained in the lease, Y promises to restore the property to its original condition at the end of the strip mining operation. Y fails to keep that promise, and X sues. Testimony produced at trial indicates that the restoration work would involve the moving of many thousands of cubic yards of dirt at a cost of $20,000. The difference between the present market value of the farm and what its value would have been if defendant had done the restoration work is only $3,000. There is a split of authority as to the appropriate measure of damages in such cases. However, some courts which have awarded the "cost of completing performance" measure have noted that to do otherwise would offer a financial inducement to future persons making substantial alterations on leased premises to intentionally breach their promises to restore the leased property to its original condition.

(d) Recovery of Consequential Damages

The "gain prevented" may include more than the present value of the promised performance itself. Defendant's breach may also prevent the making of additional gains and/or profits from other, more remote, transactions. Recovery of expectation damages will include these "consequential damages" but only if plaintiff can meet the requirements of foreseeability (§ 1.3, infra), causation (§ 1.4, infra) and reasonable certainty (§ 1.5, infra).

EXAMPLE. X and Y enter into a contract for the sale of 1000 pounds of coffee by X to Y at $2 per pound. X repudiates the contract before delivery and before Y has paid any part of the price. On the day Y learns of the breach the wholesale market price for coffee is $2.50 per pound. The net amount of direct gains prevented in this case is $500. Suppose, however, that X knew that Y intended to resell the coffee, by the cup, at his well established coffee shop. Suppose, further, that coffee is very scarce and that X had reason to know that because no other large supply of coffee would be readily available to Y, Y would be forced to close his coffee shop for two months. Subject to the rules set forth in §§ 1.3 through 1.5, X may be liable for the profits which were prevented because of Y's being forced to close the shop. (Rules governing recovery of consequential damages in contracts for the sale of goods are discussed in Chapters Five and Six infra).

(e) Recovery of Damages for Mental Suffering

As was discussed in subsection (a), supra, the formula for measuring the loss of bargain includes both gains prevented and losses suffered. In general, the term "losses suffered" does not include mental suffering. There are, however, two exceptions to this rule: (1) Where the mental suffering accompanies bodily injury, such as in a breach of warranty case; and (2) where the mental suffering was caused by an intentional or reckless breach of contract to render a service of such a character that defendant had reason to know that the breach might cause psychological anguish.

EXAMPLE 1. X's child, who lived in New York, dies while in California. X contracts with Y Airline for the transportation of the body back to New York for purposes of burial. Y's agent, who is responsible for placing the body on the airplane, becomes intoxicated, and recklessly misplaces the body, which is never found. In an action for breach of contract, X's mental suffering may be included among the "losses suffered" for which expectation damages will be awarded.

EXAMPLE 2. X, who is a guest at Y's exclusive hotel, is wrongfully ejected from the hotel dining room by Y's agent, in breach of Y's contract with X. Without any good reason, and in front of a roomful of dinner guests, Y's agent announces that X is a "pornographer and a molester of small children." After the statute of limitations for tort actions has expired, X sues Y for breach of contract. X's mental suffering is a fact that will be considered in awarding damages.

(f) Punitive Damages

Damages are punitive when they are assessed for the purpose of punishing the defendant or as an example to others, and are in excess of plaintiff's actual loss of bargain. Under the older case law, it was a cardinal rule that punitive damages were not recoverable in actions for breach of contract. There were many instances in which certain elements in plaintiff's recovery seemed to be punitive in nature; but those damages were always assessed under the theory that they were "losses suffered" by plaintiff and hence part of his expectation interest. (See e. g. the "mental suffering" examples in the immediately preceding paragraphs). Under the modern case law, however, there are two instances in which punitive damages may be recoverable. (1) Where the breach is, or is accompanied by, a tort which is maliciously or recklessly committed; (2) where the breach, although not constituting or accompanied by a tort, is a malicious or reckless breach of fiduciary duty.

EXAMPLE 1. Lessor and Lessee enter into a lease agreement. In addition to its other clauses, the lease contains a covenant by Lessor that Lessee shall be allowed to enjoy "quiet and exclusive use of the premises." In violation of the agreement, Lessor attempts to raise Lessee's rent. When this attempt proves unsuccessful, Lessor breaks into the premises at night when Lessee is not present and changes the locks on the door. The purpose of this act is to harass Lessee by denying him access to the premises. Because Lessor's breach of the lease contract constitutes a malicious tort (forcible entry and detainer) Lessee may be entitled to recover punitive damages.

EXAMPLE 2. Homeowner and realtor enter into a contract whereby homeowner conveys his home to realtor in exchange for a new one. Realtor breaches certain portions of the contract. As a result of that breach, which consists of a major misrepresentation by realtor, owner receives no money or credit for his equity in his old house. Upon suit by homeowner for breach of the agreement, homeowner may be able to recover punitive damages. Regardless of whether realtor's misrepresentations contain all the elements of the tort

[23]

of fraud and deceit, they are clearly a reckless violation of the fiduciary relationship and may give rise to punitive damages.

(g) Nominal Damages

Occasionally, an "aggrieved" party will be able to establish a cause of action for breach of contract but will not be able to prove that he has suffered any actual damage. In such a case, judgment will be given for nominal damages, a very small amount awarded without regard to actual injury for the purpose of symbolically vindicating the "wrong" done to plaintiff.

EXAMPLE. Author and publisher enter into a contract in which publisher agrees to publish author's book and pay author royalties based on a percentage of the sales. Publisher repudiates the agreement and refuses to publish the book. At trial author fails to provide a foundation for a reasonably certain estimate (see § 1.5 infra) of the amount of anticipated royalties. She also fails to allege reliance losses (see Chapter 3) suffered in performing the contract or in making necessary preparation to perform. Author is entitled to nominal damages only.

§ 1.2 The "Duty" to Mitigate Damages

Although an aggrieved plaintiff's expectation damages include both the gains prevented and the losses suffered by virtue of defendant's breach, a cardinal rule of contract damages is that plaintiff cannot recover those losses which he "could have avoided by reasonable effort, and without undue risk, expense or humiliation." Likewise, gains that plaintiff could have made by reasonable effort, and without undue risk, expense, or humiliation, by virtue of opportunities that he would not have had but for defendant's breach, are deducted from the amount that he could otherwise recover. This principle is called either the doctrine of "avoidable consequences" or the "duty to mitigate damages."

(a) Consequences of Failure to Comply with "Duty"

It is somewhat inaccurate to say that an aggrieved plaintiff has a "duty" to mitigate damages; for failure to comply with this "duty" will not defeat plaintiff's cause of action. Indeed, it will not even really affect his remedy. According to the Restatement of Contracts, "Plaintiff's remedy will be exactly the same, whether he makes the effort and avoids the harm or not. But if he fails to make the reasonable effort with the result that his harm is greater than it would otherwise have been, he cannot get judgment for this avoidable and unnecessary increase."

EXAMPLE. X, a clerk-typist, is wrongfully discharged by his employer, Y, six months before his contract would have expired. X sues Y for $5,000, the salary due him for that six month period.

At trial, Y is able to prove that immediately after being discharged, X was offered an identical position by Z, for the same six month period at a salary of $4,500. The court finds that X's rejection of that position was unreasonable and therefore constituted a violation of the "duty" to mitigate. The result of this finding is that the $4,500 gain that X *could* have made is deducted from his recovery, just as it would have been if he had actually complied with his "duty" to mitigate. That is, if X had taken the position offered by Z, X's recovery against Y would have been $500. His failure to take that position also results in a recovery against Y of $500. The effect of the mitigation doctrine is simply to preclude plaintiff from being compensated for damages ($4,500) that a reasonable person, similarly situated, would have avoided.

(b) What is Meant by "By Reasonable Effort, Without Undue Risk, Expense or Humiliation"

The doctrine of avoidable consequences is applicable only to losses which plaintiff could have avoided or gains which he could have made (1) by reasonable effort, (2) without undue risk or expense and (3) without undue humiliation. This subsection will attempt to define and illustrate each of these three components.

"By Reasonable Effort"

The doctrine requires only a "reasonable effort" to mitigate damages. It does not require that plaintiff use the most perfect means possible; nor does it require that his efforts be successful.

EXAMPLE 1. Seller and buyer enter into a contract for the sale of 15,000 tons of ore at $15 per ton payable on delivery. Seller repudiates the contract and refuses to deliver the ore. As soon as he learns of the breach, buyer, in an attempt to mitigate damages, purchases substitute ore at $18 per ton. At the time of his purchase, there is no established market price for ore. At trial, defendant introduces evidence that there were sources available from which equivalent ore could have been procured by plaintiff, had he conducted an extensive search, at $17 per ton. Consequently, argues defendant, plaintiff did not mitigate properly; and his damages should be computed on the basis of $17 per ton rather than $18. In a case with very similar facts, a federal court of appeals held that the doctrine of avoidable consequences did not require that plaintiff search for the most perfect and effective means possible of mitigating defendant's damages. All that was required was that plaintiff make *reasonable* efforts and use *reasonable* diligence in procuring at a fair price the substitute ore necessary to meet his needs. Moreover, *defendant* had the burden of proving that plaintiff did not act in a reasonable manner.

In so holding, the court stated, "the rule of mitigation may not be invoked by a contract breaker as a basis for hypercritical examination of the conduct of the injured party, or merely for the purpose of showing that the injured person might have taken steps which seemed wiser or would have been more advantageous to the defaulter. One is not obligated to exalt the interests of the defaulter to his own probable detriment."

EXAMPLE 2. X enters into a contract with Y, a licensed nurse, under the terms of which Y will live with and take care of X's aged father for a three month period while X goes on vacation. Y is to be paid $4,000 for his services. X repudiates the contract before Y performs any services or is paid any money. In an attempt to mitigate damages, Y places an advertisement in two local newspapers indicating that his private nursing services are available. No one responds to his ad; and, consequently Y is unemployed for the entire three month period. Y sues for $4,000 plus the cost of advertisements. X argues that Y did not fulfill his duty to mitigate damages. Y may recover the entire amount. The doctrine requires only that plaintiff use reasonable efforts to mitigate damages. It does not require that those efforts be successful.

"Without Undue Risk or Expense"

The doctrine of avoidable consequences does not require plaintiff to mitigate damages if, in doing so, he will incur unreasonable expenses. Moreover, he is not required to place himself in a risky situation, as by taking steps which might jeopardize his credit rating or contracts which he had made with other persons.

EXAMPLE. X and Y enter in to a contract for the sale by X to Y of a large quantity of liquor which Y intends to resell by the glass at his tavern. This purpose is known to X when he enters into the contract. After Y has paid the entire purchase price, X repudiates the contract and refuses to deliver the liquor. He also delays two months in refunding the purchase price. During this two month period, Y (since he has already paid the purchase price) does not have additional capital to invest in a second purchase of liquor. In order to make such an investment, he would have had to take out a loan from a finance company at an extremely high interest rate. Y's failure to incur this unreasonable expense will not prevent the recovery of profits which he lost by not being able to supply his customers with liquor during the two-month period.

"Without Undue Humiliation"

The prototypical case involving this facet of the rule is that of a wrongfully discharged employee who is subsequently offered a job of substantially lower rank, status, or prestige. The mitigation doctrine does not require the employee to take such a position because a natural result of doing so would be the suffering of "undue humiliation."

EXAMPLE. X, a history professor under a three year contract with Y, a prestigious university, is wrongfully discharged at the end of the second year. Because the discharge occurs in June, it is impossible for X to find another suitable professorial position for the following academic year. X sues Y for $18,000, his third year's salary. At trial, Y offers evidence that after being discharged by Y, X was offered employment by Z, an unaccredited "college" whose student body consists mainly of persons who have never graduated from high school. Had X accepted this position, his salary would have been $10,000. X can recover the entire $18,000 from Y. The mitigation doctrine does not require that a discharged employee accept a job of substantially lower rank, status and/or prestige.

(c) Accepting a Less Advantageous Contract with Defendant

There is a split of authority as to whether once defendant has breached the contract, the mitigation doctrine requires plaintiff to make another agreement with defendant if this second agreement will have the effect of minimizing damages resulting from breach of the first. Some courts have held that plaintiff must enter into this second, less advantageous, agreement with defendant if no undue humiliation, risk, expense or inconvenience is involved in making the new contract. Other courts have held that it is always inherently humiliating and/or "unduly expensive" to accede to a wrongful demand by one who has breached a contract, and that an aggrieved party, therefore, should not be required to contract again on any basis with defendant. A third position, which has been espoused by several courts, is that plaintiff must accede to the new terms only if they are "trivial" in relation to the amount of damages defendant will suffer if plaintiff refuses to deal with him.

EXAMPLE 1. Seller and buyer enter into an agreement whereby buyer will purchase goods on credit from seller. Without good reason, seller repudiates the credit agreement and demands the same price but in cash. Buyer refuses to accede to this demand, and instead purchases the goods on credit from X at a higher price. Buyer then sues seller for damages, i. e., the difference between the contract price and the "cover" price. (See Chapter 5). Seller argues that buyer could have mitigated this loss by acquiesing in the cash terms proposed by seller. On these facts, some courts have held that the mitigation doctrine does require buyer to consent to the cash terms if he can get the necessary money without suffering "undue expense." Other courts have ruled to the contrary. In ruling that the mitigation doctrine did not require this type of accession from plaintiff, one court stated:

[*31*]

"When a vendor agrees to sell on credit and then changes to a cash basis, it can mean but one thing, and that is a lack of confidence on the part of the vendor in the vendee. Surely, after that, it is humiliating to such a vendee to be required to again contract on any basis with the same vendor."

EXAMPLE 2. The X Utility Company and farmer Y have an agreement whereby X will supply Y with enough water to irrigate his crop for one year. In exchange for this service, Y is to pay X $60, payable in installments of $5 per month. X repudiates the agreement and demands the entire $60 in advance. Y refuses to go along with these terms. X shuts off the water supply, and Y's entire crop is destroyed. On similar facts, some courts have ruled that since the extra expense to plaintiff is trivial (interest on the $60 would not amount to more than a few dollars) in relation to the large amount of foreseeable resultant injury, the mitigation doctrine requires that plaintiff enter into the new agreement with the breaching defendant. Other courts have disagreed, and have allowed plaintiff to recover his entire consequential damages.

EXAMPLE 3. A previous example, which involved a wrongfully discharged employee who was offered a job by *another* institution, concluded with the principle that "the mitigation doctrine does not require that a discharged employee accept a job [from a different employer] of substantially lower rank, status, and/or prestige." The same rule holds when the wrongfully discharged employee is offered a new job by his original employer. In such cases, the courts have held that the mitigation doctrine does not require the aggrieved party to accept the new position if it will involve either undesirable personal relations, or a reduction in status or wages.

(d) Effect of Second Agreement with Defendant Upon Plaintiff's Rights for Breach of Original Agreement

The mitigation doctrine does not require plaintiff to accept a new arrangement with defendant if the new arrangement is made conditional on plaintiff's surrender of any claim he may have under the original contract.

Express Reservation of Rights

In some instances, it may be possible for plaintiff to enter into the new arrangement with defendant while expressly reserving his rights under the original contract. The Uniform Commercial Code has specifically adopted this approach. § 1-207 provides that "a party who with explicit reservation of rights performs or promises performance or assents to performance in a manner demanded or offered by the other party does not thereby prejudice the rights reserved. Such words as 'without prejudice' 'under protest' or the like are sufficient."

Implied Reservation of Rights

Occasionally, an aggrieved party will accept a new arrangement with a defaulting party and, in so doing, will neither expressly reserve nor expressly surrender his rights under the original contract. In such cases, there is a split of authority as to whether plaintiff impliedly reserves any claim he may have under the agreement which defendant has repudiated. The better reasoned view seems to be that if plaintiff enters into the new arrangement only because the repudiating defendant has indicated that the original agreement will not be performed, plaintiff's accession does *not* result in a surrender of rights under the pre-existing contract. Instead, there is an implied reservation of those rights.

Implied Reservation under the UCC

§ 2–607(2) of the UCC provides that when a seller has breached a contract by delivering non-conforming goods, the buyers "acceptance [of those goods] does not of itself impair any other remedy provided. . . . for nonconformity." In other words, if buyer mitigates his damages by entering into a substitute arrangement with seller (accepting goods which do not conform to the contract), buyer impliedly reserves his right to claim damages under the original agreement.

(e) Gains made on Other Transactions

Gains made (or which could have been made) by the aggrieved plaintiff after the breach by defendant are to be deducted from damages *if and only if* those gains would not have been possible but for defendant's breach.

EXAMPLE 1. X and Y enter into a contract whereby Y and his crew are to put aluminum siding on X's house during the first week of June for a price of $4,000. Y's "crew" consists of two other persons, and the three of them can do only one job at a time. X repudiates the contract before any work is done or any money paid. The following day Y enters into a contract with Z whereby Y and his crew will put aluminum siding on Z's house during the first week of June for $3,500. If Y and his crew had not been available during the first week of June, Z would have contracted with a different siding company. The $3,500 gain on the Y-Z contract would not have been possible but for the breach by X. Therefore, it must be deducted from Y's recovery.

EXAMPLE 2. Same facts but Y's crew is very large, and, by splitting into groups, they can do several aluminum siding jobs at once. Assuming that Y could have performed his contract with X and Z simultaneously, the $3,500 should not be deducted from Y's recovery because it is not a gain made possible by virtue of defendant's breach.

EXAMPLE 3. Seller, a car dealer, enters into a contract with buyer for the sale of a 1978 Pink Panther automobile for $6,000. Buyer repudiates the agreement, and seller immediately sells the car to X for $5,700. At the time of buyer's breach, there is only one 1978 Pink Panther on seller's lot and seller will not be able to obtain any more of these cars from the manufacturer. If the Pink Panther had not been available, X would not have purchased any automobile from seller. The $5,700 gain on seller's contract with X would not have been possible but for buyer's breach. Therefore, it must be deducted from seller's recovery. (See, *generally* UCC 2-706, which is discussed in Chapter Seven).

EXAMPLE 4. Same facts but there are more 1978 Pink Panthers on seller's lot than he will be able to dispose of. If buyer had not breached the contract, seller would have been able to perform both contracts simultaneously by selling another 1978 Pink Panther to X. In this case, the $5,700 is not deductible from seller's recovery because it is not a gain made possible by virtue of defendant's breach. [Note: In the instant EXAMPLE, seller could probably recover lost profits under UCC 2-708(2). See Chapter 7].

(f) Recovery of Costs Incurred in Efforts to Mitigate Damages

The mitigation doctrine not only *denies* recovery for losses which plaintiff could have prevented by use of reasonable efforts, but also *provides* recovery for the expenses which plaintiff incurs in making such efforts. Such expenditures will be included as damages as long as they are *reasonable* at the time they are made. They need not be successful, and may be recoverable even though hindsight reveals that they have actually increased, rather than diminished, damages.

EXAMPLE. X and Y enter into a contract for the sale of steel which Y plans to use in the construction of a bridge. Delivery is to take place on June 1. In breach of the contract, X delays delivery until October 1. At the time of contracting, X has reason to know that the erection of the steel girders will be followed by the pouring of concrete; that concrete cannot be poured in freezing weather; and consequently that any delay in delivery of the steel might force postponement of the work until spring, which would result in substantial losses to Y. When Y receives the delayed delivery of the steel, he immediately erects the girders and then embarks on a crash program, including overtime labor and other expenses, to pour the concrete before winter. These expenses, incurred in an effort to avoid the consequences of postponing the work until spring, are recoverable even though it turns out that the winter is an unusually mild one and the concrete could have been poured at any time. All that is necessary is that Y's efforts be reasonable at the time they are made; and the burden of proving "unreasonability" is on defendant, X.

§ 1.3 Foreseeability

In awarding expectation damages, the courts will compensate plaintiff only for those injuries which were "foreseeable" or "within the contemplation of the parties" at the time the contract was made. This rule does not require that defendant actually have the resulting injury in mind at the time of contracting. "Foreseeability" does not require actual foresight but only *reason to foresee.* According to the landmark ruling in *Hadley v. Baxendale,* 9 Exch. 341 (1854), two types of injuries are deemed to be foreseeable or "within the contemplation of the parties": (a) injuries which will flow naturally from the breach in the ordinary course of events, and (b) injuries which arise from plaintiff's special needs or circumstances of which defendant has knowledge or reason to know.

(a) Injuries Which Will Flow from the Breach in the Ordinary Course of Events

When parties enter a contract, they are usually contemplating performance, not breach. Thus, it is somewhat fictional to speak of *damages* as being "within the contemplation of the parties" at the time the contract is made. Nevertheless, certain types of injuries flow so naturally from a breach that the parties will be deemed to have contemplated them, even though there may have been no actual discussion of or thought given to them.

EXAMPLE. X and Y enter into a contract whereby X is to load Y's cargo of sugar onto X's vessel and carry it to Port Z where there is a market for sugar. Y intends to sell the sugar at Port Z, and X is aware of the fact that there is a market for sugar at that port. Under the terms of the contract, the vessel is scheduled to arrive at Port Z on May 1. X, in breach of the contract, delivers the sugar to Port Z on May 20, by which time the market price for sugar has fallen. As soon as the sugar arrives at Port Z, Y sells it at the current market price. Y sues. Y can recover the difference between the market price for his sugar on May 1, and the price he actually received on May 20. X should have been able to foresee that it was Y's intention to sell the sugar at the market price prevailing on May 1. He also should have been able to foresee that the market might decline between May 1 and May 20. Such circumstances occur frequently and are "in the usual course of things." It is, therefore, "within the contemplation of the parties" that late delivery of the goods might deprive B of an anticipated gain. X is liable for this "consequential damage" suffered by Y.

*(b) Injuries Which Arise from Plaintiff's Special
Needs or Circumstances, of Which Defendant
Has Knowledge or Reason to Know*

Injuries which do not flow "naturally" from the
breach in the usual course of events are, nevertheless, compensable, if at the time of contracting,
defendant had knowledge or reason to know of
special circumstances which would give rise to
such losses. Under the majority rule, the special
circumstances need not be communicated by the
plaintiff to the defendant. It is sufficient that
defendant had knowledge or reason to know of
them.

EXAMPLE 1. X, who wishes to expand his
laundry business, enters into a contract with Y
whereby Y will deliver and install a new boiler at
X's place of business on June 1. Although there is
no express discussion of the matter, Y has reason
to know that X's business expansion cannot take
place until the new boiler is received and installed.
In breach of the contract, Y delivers and installs
the boiler on November 1 instead of June 1.
Assuming that foreseeability of damages is the
only issue involved, X will be able to recover from
Y the business profits which he lost during the
period between June 1 and November 1.

EXAMPLE 2. X's mill is stopped by a breakage
in a crank shaft. X enters into a contract with Y,
a carrier, to have the shaft carried to the manufacturer for repair. Y is not told that the mill will

be stopped until the shaft is repaired, nor does he have reason to believe that this is the case. In breach of the contract, Y delays in delivering the shaft. As a result, X loses business profits because of the stoppage of the mill. C cannot recover the lost profits because Y did not know or have reason to know that his delay in delivering the shaft would cause X to lose profits.

§ 1.4   Causation

Damages are not recoverable unless they are in fact caused by defendant's breach. In contract law, the major causation problem occurs when defendant's breach is only one of two or more factors leading to plaintiff's injury. In such cases, the majority rule is that defendant's breach need not be the only factor which has caused plaintiff's damages. Instead, the causation requirement is met if defendant's breach is a "substantial factor" in bringing about the injury. In determining whether defendant's breach is a substantial factor, the courts will consider both the number of other factors which were operative, and the extent of the effect which each (including defendant's breach) had in bringing about plaintiff's losses.

EXAMPLE. Seller and buyer enter into a contract for the sale of webbing which buyer intends to use in manufacturing army leggings. Buyer is already under a contract to sell the leggings to the Army. Seller fails to deliver the webbing, and buyer is not able to obtain equivalent materials from any other source. As a result of her failure to manufacture and deliver the leggings, buyer loses her contract with the Army. Buyer sues seller for the profits which she has lost on the Army contract. At trial, seller is able to prove that Z Zipper Company also breached its contract with buyer in that it failed to deliver zippers needed for the leggings. It is not clear whether buyer could have procured zippers from another source. Seller also produces evidence that there was a two-week strike at buyer's plant which would have delayed (but not permanently halted) buyer's manufacture of the leggings. Buyer would probably be able to recover her losses on the Army contract from seller. Considering both the number of others factors which were operative and the extent of the effect produced by each, the court would probably hold that seller's breach was a "substantial factor" in bringing about buyer's loss of the Army contract.

§ 1.5 Reasonable Certainty

Expectation damages are recoverable only to the extent that their amount can be estimated with "reasonable certainty." Those damages which do not meet the "reasonable certainty" requirement are said to be "speculative" and, hence, not recoverable.

(a) Applicability to Consequential Damages

The issue of certainty of damages arises most frequently when plaintiff is seeking compensation for consequential damages—losses on transactions other than the transaction which was the subject of the breach. (See § 1.1(d) supra).

EXAMPLE 1. X and Y enter into a contract for the sale by X to Y of Rotgut bourbon at four dollars per quart. Y plans to use the Rotgut for home consumption. X breaches the contract by refusing to deliver. At the time Y learns of the breach, the market price for Rotgut bourbon is six dollars per quart. Absent other relevant factors, this case does not raise a problem involving certainty of damages. It is clear that Y has suffered expectation damages in the amount of two dollars per quart. [See UCC 2-713, which is discussed in Chapter Five].

EXAMPLE 2. X and Y enter into a contract for the sale by X to Y of a large quantity of Rotgut bourbon at four dollars per quart. X breaches the contract by refusing to deliver. At the time the contract was made, X had reason to know that Y intended to resell the Rotgut by the glass, along with other beverages, at his tavern. X also knew that Y could not obtain a supply of Rotgut or a comparable substitute from any other source. X may be liable for the profits which Y would have made on the resale of Rotgut. However, it is with respect to the gains from these latter transactions that the issue of certainty arises. Y must establish with reasonable certainty: (1) that he would have, in fact, made profits from the resale of Rotgut at his tavern (perhaps, for example, he can show that many of his pre-existing customers went elsewhere to drink Rotgut); and (2) the approximate amount of such profits.

(b) Distinguishing "Speculative" Damages from Those Which Are "Reasonably Certain"

The term "reasonable certainty" is incapable of definition. The difference between damages which are "speculative" (and hence not recoverable) and those which meet the requirement of "reasonable certainty" is one of degree only. In some jurisdictions, the requirement of certainty is applied very stringently, and something approaching mathematical precision is required in establishing proof of damages. The modern trend, however, is that the requirement should be liberally and flexibly applied. Under that view "reasonable certainty" requires nothing more than an approximate estimate of the amount of damages.

(c) New Versus Already Established Businesses

In general, if defendant's breach has prevented plaintiff from operating an already established business, the amount of lost profits can often be proved with "reasonable certainty." On the other hand, if defendant's breach has prevented plaintiff from opening a new business or producing a one-of-a-kind event or entertainment, the amount of profits thereby prevented is usually held to be speculative and therefore not recoverable.

EXAMPLE 1. X and Y enter into a lease agreement whereby Y agrees to lease a building in Northern Suburbia to X for the operation of a grocery store for a five year period, beginning on July 1, 1975. X takes possession on that date and operates the store for a period of four years. On July 1, 1979, Y, in breach of the contract, evicts X from the premises. X sues Y for lost profits for the period from July 1, 1979 to July 1, 1980. At trial, he is able to prove that his net profits during the previous four years averaged $25,000 per year. Unless Y can produce evidence negating the notion that the fifth year would have been as profitable for X, X will be able to recover lost profits from Y. Although there is no absolute guarantee that X would have earned $25,000 in profits during the fifth year, his past profits provide a basis for making an approximate estimate of the amount of damages suffered.

EXAMPLE 2. X and Y enter into a lease agreement whereby Y agrees to lease a building in Northern Suburbia to X for the operation of a grocery store for a five year period beginning on July 1, 1975. On June 15, 1975, Y repudiates the agreement with X and instead leases the premises to Z who subsequently operates a grocery store there from July 1, 1975 to June 30, 1980. X sues Y. At trial X is able to prove that: (1) for the past ten years X has operated a grocery store in *Southern* Suburbia and has earned net profits of $20,000 per year from that operation; (2) between July 1, 1975 and June 30, 1980, when Z operated a grocery store in the building that was the subject of the broken contract, she earned net profits of $30,000 per year. X will probably not be able to recover lost business profits from Y. Neither the evidence of X's profits from a similar business located elsewhere, nor the evidence of Z's earnings from a similar business located in the premises which were the subject of the broken contract, provides a basis for making an approximate estimate of the profits which X has lost by being prevented from operating a grocery store on Y's premises. This does not necessarily mean, however, that X will have *no* recovery against Y. [See subsection (d) infra for alternative measures of recovery, when lost profits cannot be established with "reasonable certainty."]

(d) *Alternative Measures of Recovery*

When lost profits cannot be approximated with reasonable certainty, it does not follow that the aggrieved party will be denied relief altogether. There are at least three alternative measures of recovery which may be available: (1) the rental value of the property which was the subject of the broken agreement; (2) the value of the chance or opportunity which was lost because of defendant's breach; (3) reliance damages [see Chapter 3, § 3.1 (a)].

Rental Value of the Property

Where the breach is one which prevents the use of property from which profits might have been earned but those profits cannot be estimated with reasonable certainty, one alternative measure of recovery is the rental value of the property.

EXAMPLE. Vendor and Vendee enter into a contract for the sale of real property on which Vendee intends to operate a tavern. The sale price is $100,000; title, possession, and the purchase price are all to pass on January 2, 1978. In breach of the contract, Vendor refuses to tender title or possession until December 2, 1978, at which time Vendee accepts the deed and pays the purchase price. On December 4, 1978, Vendee is informed that a zoning bill pending in the state legislature will, if passed, prohibit the operation of a tavern on the premises. On December 8, 1978, Vendee sells the property to Bud's Bakery for $100,000. Vendee sues Vendor, claiming that he was deprived of profits from the proposed tavern during the eleven month period between January 2 and December 2. Vendee will not be able to recover lost profits because there is no basis for estimating them with "reasonable certainty." However, Vendee may be able to recover the rental value of the property between January 2 and December 2; for, had he acquired title on January 2, he could have chosen not to operate a tavern but instead to rent out the property. Of course, from this measure of damages a deduction would have to be made for the gains made possible by virtue of the breach, i. e., the amount of interest which Vendee gained by being able to retain his $100,000 from January 2 to December 2.

Value of the Lost Opportunity or Chance

In some contracts, the performance promised by one of the parties is aleatory, which means that it is conditional on the happening of an event which is out of the control of the parties and dependent either on chance or on the exercise of discretion by a third party. If defendant breaches an aleatory promise, it is impossible to assess plaintiff's damages because it is unknown whether the fortuitous event would have ever occurred. If it would not have occurred, defendant would have had no duty to perform. In such a case, defendant's repudiation of the agreement would not result in any actual injury to plaintiff. On the other hand, if the fortuitous event would have occurred, defendant would have had the duty to perform fully.

Thus, in broken aleatory agreements, it is not the *amount* of damages which is uncertain but rather the *existence* of damage. In such cases, plaintiff *is* allowed damages, and the measure of recovery is the value of the chance or opportunity which is prevented because of defendant's breach.

EXAMPLE 1.   X is one of twenty semi-finalists in Y's puzzle contest. According to the terms of the contract which each entrant has signed, the entries are to be judged by Z, a puzzle expert, whose decisions are to be final. The four "best" entries are to win $50,000 each; and the other 16 contestants will win nothing. Y breaches his contract with X by misplacing X's entry and consequently failing to give it to Z to be judged along with the other 19 entries. In an action by X against Y for breach of contract, the jury awards X $10,000 in damages. Y appeals on the grounds that X's damages are too "speculative" to be recoverable. The verdict in favor of X will be affirmed. Although it is uncertain whether Y's breach resulted in *any* injury to X, the *chance* of winning had value which the jury could assess by taking into account all relevant factors including the law of averages. X had a 20% chance of winning. Therefore, it is not unreasonable for the jury to conclude that the value of the chance is 20% of the $50,000 prize, or $10,000.

EXAMPLE 2.   Landowner contracts with Driller for the drilling of an exploratory oil well on Landowner's property. After learning that other drilling in surrounding areas has resulted in a series of dry holes, Driller repudiates his contract with Landowner. Landowner, unable to find any other skilled person to do the work, sues Driller for breach of contract. Driller alleges that damages are purely speculative and therefore not recoverable. In some cases such as this, the courts have allowed the jury to arrive at an estimate of the value of the chance of which plaintiff was deprived because of defendant's breach. This will obviously involve a forecast of what, if any, the well's production would have been. In arriving at its estimate of the value of the prevented opportunity, the jury must take into account all relevant factors, including the fact that drilling in surrounding areas has failed to result in a productive well. (It should be noted that the agreement between Landowner and Driller is not strictly aleatory. Driller's *duty to perform* is not conditional on the happening of a fortuitous event. However, the existence of injury to Landowner *is* conditional on the occurrence of a fortuitous event).

CHAPTER 2

RESTITUTION

The remedy of restitution is based on the theory that a person who has been unjustly enriched at the expense of another should be required to return to that other person the value of the benefits that were unjustly obtained.

§ 2.1 History of Restitution

Historically, the remedy of restitution cannot be categorized as either strictly "equitable" or strictly "legal"; it was decreed by both judges and chancellors as circumstances warranted. At common law, restitutionary relief was available through the action of assumpsit. The most frequent counts were for "money had and received" (when the plaintiff's performance had been the tender of money), "goods sold and delivered"—also known as "quantum valebant"—(when performance had been the delivery of goods and chattels), and "quantum meruit" (when performance had been provision of work or services). In cases where legal relief was inadequate, the plaintiff could elect to bring an action for "recission and restitution" before the Chancellor in Equity.

§ 2.2 Difference Between Restitutionary Relief and Expectation Damages

When a contract has been breached, the remedy of expectation damages attempts to place the injured party in as good a position as he would have been in had the contract been fully performed—to give that party the "benefit of his bargain." However, in some circumstances, it is more advantageous for the injured party to seek a return to the pre-contract position or *status quo ante*. In such cases the remedy of restitution may be appropriate. When the aggrieved party has partially performed by conferring something of value upon the defendant, a restitutionary judgment will serve to "undo" the contract by returning to the injured party the value of his performance, thus placing him in the position he would have been in if he had never entered into the contract.

Given the scope of recoverable damages under the "loss of bargain" (or "expectation") formula, one might be tempted to ask: why seek restitution? If a plaintiff believes that she would have profited from the full performance of her contract, she will, of course, desire to recover the lost profit through a suit for expectation damages. But, not all bargains produce profitable results; for example, there might be a post-contract decline in the market value of defendant's performance, or plaintiff might have been a poor bargainer. If full performance would have resulted in a net loss to the plaintiff, restitution—which will often return plaintiff to the pre-contract position—is a remedy which is preferable to expectation. In such a case, the injured party will have the good fortune to escape a bad bargain and, consequently, to recover more than she would have gained (i. e. a net loss) had the contract not been breached.

EXAMPLE. Builder X contracts with Owner Y to build a house on Y's land for $50,000, payable on completion. Due to a poor job of estimating her costs, X soon discovers that it will cost her $65,000 to fulfill the contract. Fortunately for X, however, after she has partly performed, Y finds that he cannot afford the house and decides to cut his losses by repudiating the contract. X's expectation in this instance is a net *loss* of $15,000. X is the injured party, however, so she has the option of disregarding the contract price and suing for the value of her services in an action for restitution. If X is able to demonstrate that the value of the labor and materials furnished thus far is $20,000, she will be able to recover that amount (a return to the *status quo ante*) instead of suffering losses on the contract.

§ 2.3 Scope of Restitution Outside the Area of Contract Law

Unjust enrichment occurs in many situations outside the area of contract law. For example, in tort, plaintiff is sometimes entitled to restitution

[*53*]

of the amount by which defendant has been unjustly enriched by virtue of his tortious conduct. Thus, restitution may be an appropriate form of relief for such torts as conversion, misrepresentation, and a number of commercial torts. The subject of restitution as a remedy for these and other wrongs, however, is outside the scope of this work.

§ 2.4 Scope of Restitution as a Remedy for Breach of Contract

In contract law, restitution is often the remedy of choice for a party who is seeking relief *not* because the defendant has breached the contract but because the contract is contaminated by some defect which renders it a nullity. For example, restitution is often decreed when there has been a mistake in the formation or performance of an agreement. That topic is explored in Chapters 11 and 13. The present chapter, however, is limited to a discussion of restitution as a remedy for *breach*. It explores the four most frequently occurring situations in which restitution may be the remedy of choice, to wit: (a) Restitution is sometimes simply an alternative to expectation damages when defendant has breached an enforceable contract; (b) Restitution may be available when defendant has breached a contract which is unenforceable because of the existence of a valid defense such as the Statute of Frauds; (c) Restitution may be available when *plaintiff* (rather than defendant) is in breach of the contract; and, (d) There are some situations in which no actual contract exists but plaintiff has provided something of value to defendant under circumstances where social policy demands that plaintiff be compensated. In such cases, the courts will create a "contract implied in law" ("quasi-contract") and grant restitutionary relief.

(a) *Restitution as an Alternative Remedy to Expectation Damages for Defendant's Breach of an Enforceable Contract*

Restitution is usually available as a remedy for breach of an enforceable contract when three elements coalesce: (1) The defendant's breach is a "material" one; (2) The plaintiff has partially performed the contract; and (3) The plaintiff's partial performance has been received by the defendant. In such cases, an action for restitution will enable the injured party to obtain compensation for the reasonable value of his performance. The remainder of subsection (a) will examine the three aforementioned elements as well as several other issues which frequently arise when restitution is sought in lieu of expectation as a remedy for defendant's breach of an enforceable contract.

Requirement That the Breach Be "Material"

A "material" breach is one which goes to the "essence" of the contract. Usually, the breach must be of such a nature that it will either actually prevent further performance of the contract by the plaintiff or will provide a valid defense for plaintiff's failure to continue performance.

EXAMPLE.   Builder and Logger sign a contract which provides that Logger shall cut 1,000 acres of timber in consideration for Builder's promise to pay $100 per acre and to transport the timber away from the work site.   After both parties have completed approximately half the work, Builder negligently fails to remove five acres of the cut timber on time, resulting in a short delay of Logger's operation.   Logger may have a right of action for damages resulting from the delay, but an action in restitution for the value of his services to date would not succeed as the breach is only a minor one.

Plaintiff's Partial Performance: Problems of Valuation

If the plaintiff has parted with a sum of money or with goods which have an established market value, valuation of plaintiff's part performance does not present a problem.   The money or the value of the goods can simply be returned and the transaction "undone."   More frequently, however, the problem is of greater complexity, particularly when the plaintiff's performance was the rendering of services.   In such cases, restitution is attained through a money judgment for the "reasonable value" of the services. This requires the establishment of standards for judging that value.

Determining Value of Services Rendered When the Services Were Part of the Performance Bargained for

If the services rendered were part of the performance bargained for, the defendant will be assumed to have received a benefit—the value of which is determined by the market value of the services. In ascertaining "market value" the courts generally look to the amount for which such services could be purchased from plaintiff or other persons (real or hypothetical) at the time the performance was rendered. Evidential requirements for establishing market value are discussed in Chapter One, at § 1.1(b). It is important to note that it is not necessary that there be any *actual* increase in the pre-existing wealth of defendant.

EXAMPLE. Painter contracts with Owner to paint Owner's house purple, for a fee of $2,000. After Painter has completed 10% of the work, Owner changes his mind and repudiates the contract. Painter sues for restitution and proves that the market value of his services to date is $300. Owner counters by demonstrating that because his house is now 10% purple and 90% yellow, its market value has actually *decreased*. As Painter's performance was the performance bargained for in the contract, he may recover the reasonable value of his labor ($300) even though there has been no actual increase in Owner's pre-existing wealth.

Non-Receipt by Defendant: Determining the Value of "Unbargained for" Reliance Costs Which Were Incurred in Preparation to Perform

As a general rule, plaintiff's expenses incurred in preparation for his performance and/or in reliance upon the defendant's promise to perform are not assumed to be "received" by the defendant and hence are not recoverable in an action for restitution. If, however, the defendant has received an actual benefit from the plaintiff's reliance expenditures, the plaintiff may recover the benefit, which will be measured by the actual increase in the defendant's net wealth.

EXAMPLE 1. Owner contracts with Mason for the construction of a stone wall at a price of $30.00 per yard, with Mason to provide all necessary materials. Mason also owns a quarrying business and decides to excavate the necessary stone rather than to purchase it. After substantial excavation has been accomplished, Owner repudiates. Although Owner's breach would give rise to an action by Mason for *expectation* damages, an action for restitution would not be successful. The contract called only for the erection of a wall; owner neither bargained for nor received any benefit from Mason's excavation. The quarrying is considered a mere "reliance cost" or preparation for performance.

EXAMPLE 2. If, in the above fact situation, Mason excavated the stone from a quarry owned and operated by Owner, the result might be different. If Mason's labor has provided Owner with an actual benefit, then Mason will be entitled to restitution for the actual value of his work to Owner. This will be the result even though Mason's excavation work is not considered part of the "bargained for" performance.

Contracts for Delivery of a Manufactured Item

In some jurisdictions, if the performance required by the contract is the manufacture, completion and delivery of a finished article, plaintiff has no remedy by way of restitution for the value of his labor if defendant wrongfully prevents completion and delivery. Under this view, defendant has not bargained for plaintiff's services but only for a finished item. In other jurisdictions, however, a contract for the delivery of a manufactured article is viewed as a contract for the services and expertise of the particular manufacturer. Thus, a number of courts have allowed restitution for the value of labor expended in part performance prior to the defendant's breach.

EXAMPLE. In one often criticized decision, *Acme Process Equipment v. United States*, 171

Ct.Cl. 251, 347 F.2d 509 (1965), rev'd on other grounds 385 U.S. 138 (1966), the United States had contracted with Acme for the manufacture and delivery of recoilless rifles at a specified unit price. When the government breached the contract, Acme's costs were far in excess of the contract price per unit. Acme sued for restitution of its actual costs on the theory that the government had contracted not only for the finished product, but for its manufacture by Acme with an eye toward expanding the base of available defense contractors. The Court of Claims granted Acme's claim for restitution and awarded the company the value of its services "measured by what [Acme] could have got for them in the market, and not by their benefit to the [government]." As there was no way of determining such market value (due to the limited market for recoilless rifles), the court used Acme's cost of performance as a basis for the award and remanded the case to the Trial Commissioner to determine if those costs were reasonable.

Effect of the Contract Price on Restitutionary Recovery

There is a split of authority as to whether the amount recoverable in restitution is controlled by the contract price. In the majority of jurisdictions, the extent of recovery is controlled totally by the "objectively" determined reasonable value of the performance rendered. The contract price is relevant only to the extent that the contract provides evidence as to the value the parties placed on performance. Some jurisdictions have modified the majority rule by setting the *total* contract price (not the prorated price) as a ceiling on recovery, apparently believing it unjust to expose a defendant to liability of an extent not contemplated when the contract was entered. In another minority of jurisdictions, recovery in restitution is controlled by the pro-rated rate set in the contract which has been breached. Thus, if plaintiff has completed half the work contracted for when the contract is breached, an action for restitution would allow recovery of no more than half the total contract price, irrespective of the actual value of plaintiff's labor.

EXAMPLE. Attorney "A" contracts to handle a business matter for a flat fee of $5,000. The matter turns out to be more complicated than expected, and A has already spent 120 hours when he is wrongfully discharged. At the time of discharge there is an estimated one-fourth of the work still to be completed. The court finds that the value of A's work is $50 per hour and that he has therefore rendered $6,000 worth of service. Most courts would allow A to recover $6,000. A minority would limit his recovery to the $5,000 contract price. Still another minority would hold A to the pro-rated contract price of $3,750.

Effect of Full Performance by Plaintiff

If the plaintiff has fully performed and the only remaining obligation of the defendant is the payment of a liquidated sum of money, plaintiff will be limited to suing for his expectation damages —the liquidated sum which is due. A suit for restitution based on the value of plaintiff's services is usually barred. Thus, ironically, in the immediately preceding example, if attorney "A" completed all the contracted-for services, few, if any, jurisdictions would allow him to recover the $6,000 value of his work; his recovery would be limited to the contract price of $5,000.

When plaintiff has fully performed and the consideration due him is something other than a fixed sum of money, such as provision of specific goods, services, or land, the result might be different. In such cases, there is a split of authority. A majority of courts will allow a suit for restitution of the value of the plaintiff's performance. A minority will limit recovery to "loss of bargain"—the value of the consideration promised by the defendant.

EXAMPLE 1. Attorney agrees with Client to handle specified legal matters for a lump sum of $600. The task is more difficult than anticipated and Attorney fully performs the services which have an actual value of $1,000. Upon completion, Client breaches by refusing to pay his bill. Recovery will be limited to $600; Attorney may not sue for restitution of the higher actual value of his services.

EXAMPLE 2. If, in the above fact situation, Attorney contracted to work in exchange for 60 shares of stock in Client's firm, each share having a value of $10.00, the result might be different. In a majority of jurisdictions Attorney may sue for restitution and recover $1,000. In a minority, he will be restricted to his expectation of $600.

Effect of Plaintiff's Full Performance Through Payment of Monies

Plaintiff's full performance is not a bar to a restitution action when that entire performance consists only of the payment of money. Plaintiff may recover all money paid, even if she would have suffered a loss through full performance of the contract by the defendant.

EXAMPLE. S agrees to deliver to B 2,000 barrels of flour on May 1st, at a price of $10.00 per barrel. B pays the full $20,000 in advance. When S fails to deliver the flour, B sues for restitution of her payment. S argues that the price of flour on May 1st had dropped to $7.00 per barrel and that therefore B would have suffered a $6,000 loss through S's full performance of the contract. S argues that the $6,000 loss should be deducted from B's recovery and that B should be entitled to a return of only $14,000—the value of the flour on

May 1st. S's argument will fail and B will recover the entire $20,000. The result is the same at common law and under the Uniform Commercial Code. 2-711(1). (See § 5.1 infra)

Divisible Contracts: Contracts Capable of Apportionment

For purposes of this discussion, a divisible contract is a contract which can be divided into a series of performances, each of which is identified with a definitely apportioned part of the total consideration. In such cases, each performance (and its corresponding consideration) is treated as a separate contract for purposes of determining the availability of restitution. Therefore, if plaintiff has performed one or more of the contemplated performances, and the consideration apportioned to those performances is a liquidated sum of money, no right to restitution will exist. However, the fact that the contract established a unit rate of payment does not necessarily make it "divisible" for purposes of the availability of restitution. The unit rate may represent only the average value of a series of performances with widely disparate values. In such cases, it cannot be said that each of plaintiff's performances is identified with a definitely apportioned part of the consideration. Whether a contract is to be considered "entire" or "divisible" depends on the intention of the parties, which, in turn, is determined by examining the language of the contract, the method by which payment is received, and all other relevant circumstances.

EXAMPLE 1. Contractor agrees with Owner to construct 35 houses for a total price of $3,500,000. The contract provides for different types of houses, each with an explicitly established price. Each house is financed through a separate mortgage, and payment is to be made for each house separately. Owner breaches after 23 houses have been completed. The contract would probably be considered divisible, and Contractor would be limited to an action for expectation damages. Since Contractor has "fully performed" with respect to the 23 houses, the amount due him for completing those houses is a liquidated debt—which bars a suit for restitution. Since he has not performed any services with respect to the remaining 12 houses, he is likewise limited to expectation damages for breach of that portion of the contract.

EXAMPLE 2. X contracts to do 1,000 meters of excavating at $10.00 per meter. The work is not of uniform difficulty. In fact, it is contemplated that it will take approximately 75% of the estimated work period to excavate the first 200 meters. After X has completed the most difficult part of the excavation, his employer repudiates. The contract should not be considered divisible and X should be permitted to seek restitution for the value of his labor.

Restoration: Plaintiff's Return Of Any Performance Received from Defendant

Because one of the functions of restitution is the return of the parties to their pre-contract position, any performance of value received by the plaintiff from the defendant must be returned by plaintiff as a prerequisite to recovery. This is referred to as a "tender of restoration." Generally, if the plaintiff has received land, goods, or other property he must promptly, upon learning of the breach, return or offer to return that property in a condition substantially as good as when he received it.

Restoration in Situations Where a Literal "Return" of Defendant's Performance is Impossible

In some situations, it will not be possible for plaintiff to return to defendant the performance which defendant has rendered. For example, defendant's performance may have been labor or services, or it may have been the tender of property which plaintiff has resold prior to learning of defendant's breach. In such cases, restitution will be allowed if the performance which plaintiff has received can be effectively valued and that value credited against the plaintiff's recovery. The burden of proving the value of the performance received rests with the plaintiff.

Restoration of Value Received by Insured While Insurance Policy is in Force

When an insurance company wrongfully repudiates a policy, the insured may seek restitution of premiums paid, plus interest, as an alternative to an action for reinstatement of the policy and/or damages. A problem arises in determining what, if any, actual benefit accrued to the plaintiff while the policy was in force, as such benefit must be "restored" to the defendant. A majority of courts allow restitution of all premiums paid without any deduction. The theory is that since the plaintiff never had occasion to collect on the policy, she received no actual benefit. A sizeable minority deduct an actuarily determined "insurer's cost of carrying the risk" from the plaintiff's recovery. Those cases proceed on the theory that, because the insured could have enforced her right to coverage through legal action (if a loss had been incurred while the policy was in force), she did receive an actual benefit, the value of which must be restored to the defendant.

Restoration of Value Received by Plaintiff Through Use of Land or Chattels

There is a split of authority as to whether plaintiff will be barred from seeking restitution of the purchase price after he has made use of land or chattels received under a contract prior to discovery of the breach. The courts in a minority of jurisdictions hold that substantial use or occupation by the plaintiff makes return to the *status quo ante* an impossibility and thus will deny restitution. A majority of courts, however, will allow the action if the plaintiff seeks restitution within a reasonable time after learning of the breach and the value of his use is capable of estimation. In such a case, the value of plaintiff's use will be credited against his recovery. Thus if the contract was for the sale of land, the reasonable rental value of the property for the period of plaintiff's occupancy will be deducted from the purchase price recovered by plaintiff by way of restitution.

Situations Where Restoration is Not Required

As the requirement of restoration exists to promote fairness, and not to unduly hamper recovery, restoration is not necessary under the following circumstances: (1) when the performance received by plaintiff was wholly without value, (2) when the goods or property received by plaintiff have been destroyed or harmed by the defendant, or as a result of defects constituting breach of defendant's contract, or (3) when the plaintiff has received money, which can simply be credited against his recovery.

Plaintiff's Actions After Knowledge of Breach as Affecting the Right to Restitution

If the plaintiff continues his own performance after receiving knowledge that defendant has breached the contract, restitution will not be awarded. Likewise, if the plaintiff accepts a performance with knowledge that it is defective or incomplete he will usually be barred from later seeking restitution. Thus, as is the case in a suit for expectation damages, a plaintiff seeking restitution has a "duty" to mitigate damages. (See § 1.2 supra).

EXAMPLE 1. Collector delivers 15 paintings to Artist who has contracted to clean, repair, and restore them for $500. After Artist has finished work on five of the paintings, Collector repudiates the contract. Artist nevertheless continues work and finishes the remaining ten. Artist is not entitled to restitution for the value of work done after learning of Collector's repudiation.

EXAMPLE 2. A contracts to purchase B's house on the condition that it will be repainted and the furnace repaired prior to closing. When the date for closing the sale arrives, B has completed none of the work called for in the contract. A is aware of this fact, but nevertheless decides to accept B's tender of the deed and to complete the sale. A is barred from later seeking restitution of the money paid to B.

UCC Exception: Assumption of Cure under UCC 2-608(1)(a)

Under the UCC, a non-conforming tender may be accepted "on the reasonable assumption that its non-conformity would be cured" without prejudice to the right to revoke acceptance and recover the purchase price if the non-conformity is not cured. UCC 2–608(1)(a).   See Chapter 6.

Election of Remedies

Historically, expectation damages and restitution were strictly alternative remedies. It was accepted policy that an injured party would not be given both a return of the value of his performance and the value of the performance promised him.   It was proper for a plaintiff to sue alternatively for both restitution and damages, but an election was necessary before the case was submitted to the jury.

Buyers Remedies under the UCC: Election Not Required

The UCC has explicitly repudiated the "election of remedies" doctrine by allowing expectation and restitution to be awarded cumulatively.   Under UCC 2–711, when a seller breaches contract, the aggrieved buyer may recover "so much of the price as has been paid," (restitution), and may *in addition* recover expectation damages under either UCC 2–712 or 2–713 (see § 5.1(a) infra).

Specific Restitution

"Specific restitution" (restitution in specie) is an equitable decree ordering a return of property transferred by the plaintiff in part performance of a contract. The term is used in contrast to "value restitution" which provides for a money judgment reflecting the value of the plaintiff's performance. The availability of this type of relief is controlled by the requirements for the issuance of equitable decrees generally. For example, specific restitution will not be decreed if a money judgment will be adequate to do justice between the parties.

EXAMPLE. Inventor has created and patented a nuclear powered potato peeler which he believes will revolutionize the industry. After extensive negotiations, the patent is sold to Manufacturer in consideration of a 10% royalty agreement and Manufacturer's promise to use his skill in producing and marketing the product. Manufacturer produces no peelers and, in fact, commits a total breach of the contract by failing to make any use of the patent for several years. Inventor is entitled to specific restitution of the patent. Both expectation damages and "value" restitution would be inadequate remedies as any reasonable estimate of the patent's worth or the royalties obtainable through sales of peelers would be entirely speculative.

Specific Restitution of Real Property

Specific restitution of real property will generally not be granted. In denying such relief the courts have referred to a perceived "need for preserving the finality of a deed and the integrity of title to real property." This problem is not one that occurs frequently, however, because prior to transfer of the deed, title remains with the vendor who will simply be excused from performance by the vendee's breach. On the other hand, if the deed has been transferred, a suit for either specific restitution or value restitution will usually, but not always be barred by the "full performance" limitation.

EXAMPLE. Plaintiff conveys a parcel of land to Builder in return for Builder's promise to build a road over the land, which will increase the value of the remainder of plaintiff's property. Upon Builder's repudiation, plaintiff may obtain "value" restitution (the value of the land), or, in the alternative, expectation damages (the value of the road), but may not obtain specific restitution of the land. The latter remedy would not be barred by the "full performance" limitation, as Builder's return consideration (the promise to build a road) is not a liquidated debt. However, the perceived "need for observing the finality of the deed and the integrity of title to real property" would probably bar specific relief.

Transfer of Land in Consideration of Support for Life

The major exception to the rule against specific restitution of real property arises when the consideration for the transfer is a promise by the vendee-defendant to support the vendor or another for life, usually with both parties living together on the land. If the vendee/defendant fails to provide the support promised, most courts will order specific restitution through cancellation of the deed —a result dictated by the inadequacy of a money judgment in fulfilling the ends of the contract. As one court stated: "it would not do to deprive the plaintiff of his property for the rest of his life and not given him the care the defendant had promised . . ."

Specific Restitution in Sales of Goods Cases

Both at common law and under the UCC, specific restitution of goods sold is generally not available to an aggrieved seller as against a buyer in default. The law provides a seller with adequate alternative methods of securing his right to payment, such as the retention of a security interest in the goods and the availability of the conditional sales contract. Exceptions to this general rule exist in limited instances as when a cash sale is made in consideration of a check subsequently dishonored (UCC 2–511) or when a sale is made to an insolvent buyer, if certain requirements are met (UCC 2–702) (see § 8.3 infra).

*(b) Restitution of Benefits Conferred in Part Per-
formance of an Unenforceable Contract*

There are many instances in which a "contract"
is either unenforceable or voidable at the option of
one of the parties, and yet the other party has
acted (or refrained from acting) in reliance on his
belief that an enforceable contract exists. Sometimes that party's action will include the conferring of benefits. The most frequently occurring
example is when a promisor has not signed a writing sufficient to meet the requirements of the applicable statute of frauds, and the promisee finds
himself in the position of having conferred benefits
on the promisor without having any legal right to
compel payment for them under the contract.
Since retention of such benefits by the promisor
will usually be "unjust", a promisee in such circumstances will generally be entitled to restitution.

Rationale for Allowing Restitution in Statute of Frauds Cases

Provision for a restitutionary remedy in the
above-mentioned situation is consistent with the
purposes of the statute of frauds. The original
English statute was titled "An Act for the Prevention of Frauds and Perjuries", and the enactment
of such statutes represents, inter alia, a legislative
determination that the *enforcement* of certain
types of contracts without supportive writing car-
ries the risk of such frauds. If the plaintiff has

rendered a performance of value to the defendant, an action to recover that value and return the parties to their pre-contract position does not attempt "enforcement" of the contract.

Recovery of "Unbargained for" Reliance Damages under an Unenforceable Contract

As was discussed in § 2.4(a), "unbargained for" reliance damages are not recoverable in an action for restitution unless they provide an "actual benefit" to the defendant. This principle is applied by most jurisdictions to *unenforceable* contracts in the same manner as it is applied to enforceable contracts. A plaintiff under an unenforceable contract, however, lacks a "loss of bargain" remedy, and application of the "no reliance damages" principle can leave a party who has spent considerable sums in preparation for performance with no remedy at all, even though his reliance was clearly induced by the defendant's unenforceable promise. To prevent such an unjust result, a number of courts have allowed recovery for out-of-pocket reliance expenses if they were incurred at the request of the defendant. Those courts justify recovery on the ground that since the plaintiff's expenses were incurred at the request of defendant, the incurring of such expenses actually confers a benefit on defendant (albeit an intangible one). Consequently, to grant relief is simply to allow "restitution" of that benefit.

"Estoppel" Through Foreseeable Reliance

As an alternative to granting recovery of reliance costs on the immediately preceding "stretched restitution" theory, a number of courts have adopted the view that foreseeable reliance by the plaintiff on the defendant's unenforceable promise "estops" the defendant from asserting the unenforceability of the contract.

EXAMPLE. Farmer orally contracts with Owner to manage Owner's farm in Texas for one year in return for a percentage of the crops raised. The one year period is to start when Farmer arrives in Texas. In reliance on the contract, Farmer sells his home in Kentucky and at a considerable expense moves his family and belongings to Texas. As soon as Farmer arrives, Owner repudiates. The oral contract is unenforceable because it is within the "one year" provision of the statute of frauds. Farmer brings an action for restitution. In a number of jurisdictions, Farmer's moving expenses may not be recovered because those reliance costs were not part of the "bargained for" exchange and did not provide any benefit to Owner. However, some courts will allow restitutionary recovery of such costs because they were incurred at the request of Owner. Other courts will grant recovery on the theory that Farmer's foreseeable reliance estops Owner from asserting the statute of frauds.

Effect of Full Performance of an Unenforceable Contract

The rule that full performance of a contract will bar the plaintiff's right to restitution does not apply to full performance under an unenforceable contract, as the plaintiff in such a case lacks an alternative remedy. Frequently, however, the plaintiff's part or full performance will take the case out of the statute of frauds, thus rendering the contract enforceable and subject to all limitations on the right to restitution under *enforceable* contracts.

(c) Restitution as a Remedy for a Plaintiff Who Has Himself Committed a Material Breach of Contract

When the plaintiff is the party who has committed a material breach, the law excuses the defendant from any further performances under the contract, thus rendering it impossible for plaintiff to maintain a successful action for breach of contract. However, in some situations the value of plaintiff's part performance prior to plaintiff's breach exceeds the damages caused the defendant by the plaintiff's breach. When this occurs, an action for restitution can, under some circumstances, be maintained. In such cases, plaintiff will be permitted to recover the net difference between the value conferred on the defendant and the damages which defendant suffered. The law of restitution in favor of a defaulting plaintiff is something of a tangle, reflecting a tension between the desire to preserve the sanctity of contracts (and thus refrain from rewarding a plaintiff for his breach) and a desire to avoid unjust enrichment (by allowing a defendant to retain benefits which plaintiff has bestowed on him). As different courts have struck different balances (often, but not always, depending on the type of contract at issue), the availability of restitution in this situation varies greatly from jurisdiction to jurisdiction.

Necessity of Differentiating Between a "Material" and a "Non-Material" Breach

It is only where the plaintiff's breach is of such a magnitude as to excuse the defendant from further performances that the law bars an action for expectation damages by the plaintiff and limits the availability of relief, if any, to restitution. Materiality of breach is a topic which is beyond the scope of this work. In general, however, a material breach is one that goes to the "essence" of the contract or consists of a failure by one of the parties to perform a condition precedent to performance by the other. If the breach committed by the plaintiff is not "material", a refusal to perform by the defendant would itself be a breach of contract for which plaintiff may recover the full scope of available damages.

Restitution in Favor of a Defaulting Plaintiff: Three Views

Because the defaulting plaintiff is considered to be the "wrongdoer" rather than the aggrieved party, the courts are in considerable conflict as to whether to award that "wrongdoer" *any* relief, including restitution of benefits which he has conferred on the aggrieved defendant. In general, three views have been taken. First, the older, more traditional, view was characterized by an extreme reluctance to allow any relief to a "wrongdoer" who had intentionally committed a breach of contract. To allow restitution was seen as putting a premium on bad faith and lessening the sanctity of contractual obligations. Indeed, some judges found "monstrous" the idea that a plaintiff in voluntary default could use his own wrong as the basis for an action against a wholly innocent party. Thus, the statement was often made that a plaintiff in default could recover no compensation for part performance rendered, a view that still holds sway in a small number of jurisdictions.

Strict application of the common law rule against restitution in favor of a defaulting plaintiff can be harsh in the extreme and often results in huge windfall profits to the defendant. The rule also creates a somewhat anomalous situation where a party who defaults immediately finds herself in a much better position than a party who attempts and completes a significant portion of the performance bargained for. Faced with situations where enforcement of the rule would greatly and unjustly enrich the defendant, a growing number of courts have espoused a second view, characterized by the maxim that "equity abhors a forfeiture and the law does not favor it." Thus, in "appropriate cases" restitution should be allowed.

EXAMPLE. Plaintiff had agreed to work for one year in the service of Defendant for $12,000, the entire amount to be paid at the end of the year in one lump sum. Plaintiff ceased working after nine and one-half months and sued for restitution of the value of his labor. Under the old common law view, a plaintiff so situated was frequently sent away empty-handed with an admonition to perform his contractual obligations more faithfully in the future. In such a case the enrichment to the defendant is obvious and the burden on the plaintiff so out of proportion to the severity of his wrong that a minority of early common law decisions began allowing restitution. Today, a majority of courts would do so, and would allow plaintiff to recover the net difference between the value conferred on defendant and the damages which defendant has suffered.

A number of jurisdictions and the Restatement of Contracts (First) have tried to resolve this conflict of views by adopting a third position—a compromise which allows restitution in favor of a de-

[*80*]

faulting plaintiff only if the default is not "willful
and deliberate." "Willful and deliberate" means
something more than "intentional," and requires
looking at the motivation of the plaintiff. Default
solely for the purpose of escaping a losing contract
is certainly willful, and in such cases, restitutionary recovery will not be allowed. However, a
knowing default for reasons of personal hardship,
insolvency, negligence or error of judgment may
not bar recovery if the circumstances are such as
to imply a "moral justification." The line between
willful and non-willful conduct is an elusive one
and must, of necessity, turn on the facts of the
case at hand.

EXAMPLE. Builder contracts with State to repair the guardrail system on a stretch of state
highway. The contract specifications call for the
installation of 1,500 concrete posts, each to be rein-
forced with four steel rods. After completion of
the project, investigation demonstrates that only
two reinforcing rods have been used per post, a
material breach of contract which greatly weakens
the structure but does not render it valueless.
State refuses to pay for the work and Builder
brings an action for restitution. Under the Restatement view, the fact finder would look to
Builder's motivation in determining his entitlement
to restitution. If Builder knowingly cut corners on
the contract specifications to save the cost of the
additional reinforcing rods, his material breach

would clearly be willful and he would have no right to restitution. On the other hand, if the weaker posts had been inadvertently substituted as a result of Builder's negligence, the breach might be found non-willful and restitution allowed for the value of of his services offset by the costs required to bring the work up to contract specifications.

Elements of a Restitutionary Action in Favor of a Defaulting Plaintiff

As restitution relies on the unjust enrichment of the defendant, a defaulting plaintiff must show such enrichment, and its amount, with a reasonable degree of certainty. To do so, she must be able to prove (1) the extent of the defendant's damages caused by plaintiff's breach, and (2) the value of the part performance which plaintiff conferred on the defendant. If both these elements are reasonably well quantified, the plaintiff may recover the value of the net benefit her performance has conferred upon the defendant, not to exceed the pro-rated contract price. It must always be kept in mind that the defendant is the innocent party, and all doubts must be resolved in his favor.

Requirement That the Defaulting Plaintiff Demonstrate the Extent of Defendant's Damages

In most cases where a contract is breached the injured party is assumed to have suffered some damage—at a minimum, the loss of time and effort that went into forming the contract. The burden is on the defaulting plaintiff to quantify defendant's damages as a prerequisite to comparing them with the value of her part performance. If she fails to make such a showing, or the amount of damage suffered by the defendant is speculative, no recovery will be allowed.

EXAMPLE. In the guardrail example above, assuming that Builder's breach is not willful, he will still have the burden of proving the amount of damages suffered by the State by virtue of his negligence. In this instance, the amount will, in all likelihood, be quantifiable and will be measured by the costs which the state must incur in bringing the work up to contract specifications. If the state claims a larger amount of damages, the burden will be on *Builder* to establish the smaller amount.

Requirement That Plaintiff Demonstrate an Actual Benefit Conferred on Defendant

As has been previously discussed, when *defendant* is the defaulting party, an aggrieved plaintiff will often be entitled to restitution even if his part performance did not result in an actual increase in the net wealth of defendant. However, when *plaintiff* is the defaulting party, he is required not only to prove that his performance has increased defendant's actual wealth but also to quantify the amount of that increase. It is possible that a performance which is costly to plaintiff will provide no actual benefit to defendant. In such situation, because defendant is the innocent party, plaintiff will not be allowed any relief.

EXAMPLE. Architect "A" contracts with Builder "B" to produce a set of plans for B's proposed restaurant. As a result of negligence in surveying the site, the plans submitted incorporate land not owned by "B"—a material breach of the contract which renders the plans useless. The remedy of restitution is unavailable to "A" because his plans are of no actual value to "B".

Restitution on Behalf of a Defaulting Vendee in a Contract for the Sale of Land

Perhaps because of the importance of property rights in the American legal system, a number of jurisdictions still follow the old common law rule denying a defaulting plaintiff-vendee restitution of monies paid prior to breach, although many of these courts will refuse to grant restitution only if the contract expressly provides for forfeiture of monies paid.

The harshness of the common law rule has caused many courts to seize upon any plausible ground for avoiding forfeiture, such as a mutual recission or vendor's waiver of the forfeiture clause, implied by her actions subsequent to vendee's breach.

EXAMPLE. "B" contracts for the purchase of "A's" farm at a price of $24,000. The parties reside in a jurisdiction which follows the common law rule denying restitution to a vendee in default on a land sales agreement. Moreover, the contract contains an express forfeiture clause. After paying $21,000 on the purchase price, "B" commits a breach of contract by failing to make a required $500 installment payment. "A" sends "B" a letter setting forth the breach and stating, "I do hereby elect to take the property back and to rescind the contract." "B" then moves off the land and commences an action for the return of a portion of the money paid to date. In theory, "B" has no right to recovery in the action for restitution. However, the resulting injustice would be so obvious that some courts are willing to ignore the obvious intent of "A's" letter and to find that his use of the word "rescind" created an offer of mutual recission and/or an express waiver of the forfeiture provision—thus allowing "B" to recover a portion of the moneys paid. ("A", of course, will be allowed a deduction for lost use of and investment opportunities in the land during the period of "B's" occupancy).

Down Payments and Earnest Money

Virtually all courts will allow the vendor to retain any down payment or earnest money as liquidated damages for the breach, even if not expressly provided for by the contract.

Construction Contracts: Restitution on Behalf of Defaulting Contractor

The courts are split on the issue of whether to allow restitution in favor of a building contractor who is in substantial default. In jurisdictions allowing recovery, the value of the work done is often measured by taking the total contract price and subtracting the owner's cost of completing the work to contract specifications. In jurisdictions where restitution in favor of a defaulting contractor is, theoretically, not allowed, the harsh results of the rule are often mitigated by finding that the contractor's breach was "de minimus" and not a "material" breach of contract.

EXAMPLE. Builder contracts with Owner to construct a house on Owner's lot for a price of $30,000, to be paid on completion. After spending $23,000 in part performance of the contract, Builder declares bankruptcy and is unable to complete the structure. The house, though unfinished, is habitable and has a market value of $25,000. Owner decides to complete the house to specifications, which now costs $8,000, and incurs $1,000 in incidental damages due to his delay in moving in. In a jurisdiction which allows restitution in favor of a contractor in default, Builder could recover $21,000—the unpaid contract price ($30,000) minus both the cost of completion ($8,000) and the incidental damages ($1,000). In a jurisdiction which theoretically does not allow restitution, a court might find that the contractor's breach was not "material", and thus permit the same recovery.

Employment Contracts: Restitution on Behalf of Defaulting Employee

An employee in default on an employment contract has always been a sympathetic plaintiff, and even at common law a minority of jurisdictions allowed such a defaulter to sue in "quantum meruit." There has been little litigation on the subject in the last 40 years as state statutes and collective bargaining agreements have made periodic payment of wages universal. As a result, there is seldom enough money at stake to warrant litigation. If such a case were to arise today, most jurisdictions would allow restitution under any circumstances, and all would compensate a "nonwillful" defaulter. Such recovery would be dependent upon a showing of actual benefit to the employer, and subject to offset for damages caused by the breach.

Sales of Goods: The UCC Position

The UCC attempts to chart a compromise course between the various common law positions. A defaulting buyer is entitled to restitution of all monies paid as a deposit or part payment in excess of any amount provided for in a seller's liquidated damages clause. UCC 2–718(2)(a). (See Chapter 9). In the absence of a liquidated damages clause, the seller may retain "twenty percent of the value

[*87*]

of the total performance for which the buyer is obligated under the contract or $500, whichever is smaller"—with the buyer entitled to restitution of the remainder. UCC 2-718(2)(b). The "right to restitution" provided by the UCC is "subject of offset" to the extent that the seller can show (1) his entitlement to damages under other provisions of the Code, and (2) the amount or value of any benefits flowing directly or indirectly to the buyer by reason of the contract. UCC 2-718(3).

A seller in default has a right to payment at the contract rate for any goods accepted and retained by the buyer. UCC 2-607(1). Such payments may, of course, be offset by any damages caused to buyer by the breach [UCC 2-607(2)].

Defendant's Actions Subsequent to Knowledge of Default as Creating a Right to Restitution in a Defaulting Plaintiff

Even in jurisdictions which deny a defaulting plaintiff the right to restitution, such a right can be created if the defendant has accepted a part performance with knowledge that a breach of the plaintiff's duty has occurred or will occur. Acceptance of a performance under these circumstances is seen as carrying with it an implied promise to pay for value received.

EXAMPLE. Employee enters into a written contract with Employer to work for one month for a fixed sum payable at the end of the contract period. The courts of the jurisdiction have repeatedly dis-allowed restitution in favor of an employee in "willful" default on an employment contract. Upon reporting for work, Employee tells Employer that he intends to work for only three weeks. Employer then tells Employee that she considers Employee to be in breach of their contract but nevertheless allows him to work. Employee resigns as predicted and seeks restitution for the value of his three weeks of labor. Restitution will be granted as Employer accepted Employee's part performance with knowledge of the future "willful" breach.

(d) Restitution of the Value of Unsolicited Benefits Voluntarily Conferred: Quasi-Contract

There are some situations in which no actual contract exists but plaintiff has provided something of value to defendant under circumstances where social policy requires that plaintiff be compensated. In such cases, the courts will create a "contract implied in law" (also known as a "quasi-contract") and will grant restitutionary relief.

Theory of the "Contract Implied in Law"

The quasi-contract (contract implied in law) is a legal fiction which is based neither on an expressed promise by defendant to pay for the benefit received nor on conduct of defendant from which such a promise can be implied. The recipient of such a benefit (the defendant) has not solicited it, and often may have been unaware that it was being conferred upon him. In such cases, there is, of course, a lack of mutuality of assent necessary to form a contract. The contract implied in law is based, instead, on a societal judgment that certain acts should be encouraged through the provision of a mechanism to ensure compensation for their performance. Thus, the obligation to pay arises through the operation of law, not through the expressed or implied consent of the defendant.

Distinction Between "Contract Implied in Law" and "Contract Implied in Fact"

Care should be taken to avoid confusion between "contracts implied in law" and "contracts implied in fact." The "contract implied in fact" is a "true" contract which derives its existence from the mutual assent of the parties. The only difference between an express contract and a contract implied in fact is that in the latter, "mutual assent" is, in part, implied from actions rather than express words or writings. In contrast, if a contract is "implied in law," there is no mutual assent. Instead, a fictional "contract" is created for reasons of social policy.

EXAMPLE. A and B are next-door neighbors who are not on friendly terms. One day A approaches B and says, "I have decided that good fences make good neighbors. I am going to build a

ten-foot high iron fence on the boundary line of
our properties. It will cost $1,000. Will you pay
for half of it?" B smiles, and shakes hands with
A, but says nothing. After the fence is erected, A
attempts to collect $500 from B, but B refuses to
pay. A sues. If the court permits recovery, it
will be on the theory that B's conduct was a man-
ifestation of assent to A's offer—thus creating a
contract implied in fact. It would be incorrect to
label this agreement a "quasi-contract" or "contract
implied in law."

The Justified Intervenor Versus the "Officious Intermeddler."

As a general rule, the conferring of unsolicited
benefits on another does not result in the creation
of a quasi-contract. On the contrary, it is often
stated that "equity abhors an officious intermed-
dler." Consequently, the individual who confers a
benefit upon another without request can usually
not expect compensation. While the recipient of
such a benefit is sometimes "enriched," the enrichment is not deemed to be "unjust." Thus, the
chief problem in defining the scope of quasi-contractual recovery is the determination of where the
line between "justified" and "officious" intervention
lies—a determination necessarily subjective and
turning on the facts of the individual case.

The remainder of this subsection is devoted to a
discussion of the typical situations in which that
line must be drawn.

Preservation of Another's Life or Health

A person who, with intent to charge, provides emergency goods or services to another which are necessary to prevent the other from dying or suffering serious bodily harm may obtain restitution for the market value of those goods or services. This is probably the strongest case for the creation of a quasi-contract. The right to restitution exists only for those things which were immediately necessary. The emergency which creates the right to restitution limits it, and no recovery may be had for goods or services provided after the emergency has passed.

Protection of Another's Property

In rare instances, restitution may be allowed in favor of a plaintiff who acts to save another's property, but only if (1) it was necessary to take action before it was possible to obtain the owner's consent, and (2) plaintiff had no reason to believe that the owner would not consent to his actions. It appears that there are relatively few reported cases in which restitution has actually been granted for unsolicited expenditures made for the protection of another's property. Preservation of property simply does not carry as compelling a justification as does preservation of life, health, or public safety. In those rare situations in which restitution is granted, the plaintiff is usually not a "stranger" but has some connection with the property or with the owner sufficient to remove his actions from the category of "officious intermeddling."

EXAMPLE. Contractor agrees with Owner to make certain specified improvements on Owner's property while Owner is on vacation in Europe. During the period of construction, and through no fault of Contractor, the building catches fire and firemen are forced to chop a hole in the roof in order to put out the blaze. To prevent the elements from causing serious additional damage to the inside of the structure and its contents, Contractor repairs the roof at a cost of $300. Owner has left no one in charge of the property in his absence, and cannot be contacted. Contractor may receive restitution for his costs in preserving the property.

Performance of Another's Duty to Protect Public Health or Safety

Restitution will be allowed for the value of plaintiff's performance if it was immediately necessary to satisfy the requirements of public health or safety. If another person was under a legal duty to render that performance, plaintiff may recover from that person.

EXAMPLE. The XYZ Transportation Company negligently causes a barge loaded with liquid chlorine to sink in the Detroit River. Under applicable law, XYZ is under a duty to remove the

[*93*]

sunken barge but refuses to do so, claiming excessive cost and difficulties. Faced with the imminent threat that the chlorine storage tanks could rupture, and release a large cloud of very toxic chlorine gas, the government raises the barge, eliminating the hazard. The government is entitled for restitution from XYZ of the costs incurred in the performance of XYZ's legal duty.

Performance of Another's Duty to Supply Necessities to a Third Person

Restitution may be had for the performance of another's duty to provide necessities to a third person if: (1) the duty is created by statute or common law, rather than by contract; (2) there has been a breach of that duty, and (3) the plaintiff is an "appropriate intervenor"—a very subjective requirement based on the existence or nonexistence of others willing to provide the necessary goods or services.

EXAMPLE 1. Wife leaves town, abandoning her invalid husband and providing him with no means of support—a violation of both common law and statutory duty. Husband's brother gives $10,000 to Husband to enable him to afford food, housing, and necessary medical and nursing care. Assuming that Brother did not intend to make a gift of the money, his action for restitution against Wife would succeed.

EXAMPLE 2. In the above fact situation, if the necessary support had been provided by a stranger, the outcome might be different. In cases where the support provided was immediately necessary to preserve Husband's life or health, [See discussion supra], or if there existed no "appropriate" persons to provide long term support, the stranger might be entitled to restitution. However, if stranger acts with knowledge that members of Husband's family exist and might be willing to provide him with care if informed of his situation, stranger's actions might be considered "officious." The stranger would no longer be considered a justified intervenor.

Unsolicited Services of Lawyers

When the successful outcome of litigation results in unsolicited benefits being bestowed upon persons who are not parties to the lawsuit, the recipients of the benefit often will be required to make restitution of the value of the attorney's services involved in pursuing the litigation. A frequently occurring example is when an attorney hired to "break" a will sues for restitution of the value of his services from non-party heirs benefitted by his action, even though he has received the agreed upon compensation from his client. While there would seem to be no acceptable rationale for providing restitution in such circumstances, there is a split of authority on the subject, leading one commentator to note that "the case law . . . expresses a conviction, widely held among judges and lawyers, at least, that lawyers have a right that is denied to all the rest of the population, to share the wealth of strangers that their services have produced."

EXAMPLE. Attorney is hired by Nephew to contest the will of his deceased uncle, which inconveniently leaves most of the estate to charity. The contract between Attorney and Nephew provides for a 50% contingency fee arrangement. Additional relatives of the decedent refuse to join the suit. Attorney's efforts are successful, and each of six relatives receives a substantial inheritance. After collecting 50% of the Nephew's inheritance, Attorney brings an action against the five remaining relatives for a percentage of the money which they inherited as a result of his efforts. There would seem to be no theoretical justification for granting restitution; however authority is split and restitution has been both allowed and denied under similar fact situations.

Measuring the Value of Benefits Conferred Upon the Defendant

When the restitution is granted under the theory of a contract implied in law, the value of the benefit to be recovered from the defendant is measured by the reasonable value of the goods or services furnished by plaintiff, not the extent of the increase in defendant's net wealth.

EXAMPLE. A, a physician, provides emergency care to B, an unconscious patient. A's efforts are unsuccessful, and B dies without regaining consciousness. B's estate refuses to compensate A, arguing that since B never regained consciousness, he received no benefit. A sues. If the court decides that this is an appropriate case for quasi-contractual relief, A will be entitled to restitution for the reasonable value of her services.

Requirement of an "Intent to Charge" as a Prerequisite to Quasi-Contractual Recovery

Restitution will not be granted in favor of a plaintiff who, at the time the benefit was conferred, did not have an expectation of, or an intent to require, compensation. A benefit conferred without a concurrent intent to charge for it is, by definition, a gift. As with all gift transactions, the giver may not later change his mind and demand payment. The existence of an intent to require compensation is a question of fact to be determined by taking into account all relevant facets of the case, including the expense sustained by the plaintiff, the customs of the community, and the relationship of the parties.

Business Dealings and Professional Services: Presumption of an Intent to Charge

One who provides goods or services in the course of his business or profession will be presumed to intend to charge for their value. (See Example, supra, involving physician and unconscious patient).

Family Relationships: Presumption of Donative Intent

If the plaintiff has rendered services to a family member, there is usually a rebuttable presumption of donative intent. This presumption of gratuity may be rebutted by the facts of the case at hand, especially if the services provided were of a type not commonly an incident of the relationship in question.

CHAPTER 3

RELIANCE DAMAGES

The primary function of the law of contract damages is to place the injured party in as good a position as he would have been in had the contract been fully performed. This goal is achieved by awarding damages which will "compensate" plaintiff for injury to his expectation interest. (See Chapter 1). The law of contract damages, however, also has two secondary functions—protection of the restitution interest (Chapter 2) and compensation for injury to the reliance interest. As previously discussed, the restitution interest represents plaintiff's interest in recouping the benefits he has conferred on defendant prior to defendant's breach. In contrast, the reliance interest represents the detriment that plaintiff has incurred by changing his position in reliance on his belief that defendant would fulfill his part of the bargain. An award of reliance damages serves the function of returning plaintiff to the status quo ante—the position which he occupied before entering into the contract.

§ 3.1 Situations in Which an Award of Reliance Damages is Appropriate

In most breach of contract cases, the plaintiff will wish to receive the full benefit of his bargain and not merely to be returned to his pre-contract position. Thus, in the typical case, the plaintiff will seek and the court will award expectation damages. There are, however, a number of instances in which judicial relief is, or should be, limited to an award of reliance damages. These situations are described and analyzed below.

(a) Cases in Which the Requirement of "Reasonable Certainty" Precludes an Award of Expectation Damages

Expectation damages are recoverable only to the extent that their amount can be estimated with "reasonable certainty." [§ 1.5 supra]. When they cannot be so estimated, it does not follow that the aggrieved party will be denied relief altogether. There are at least three alternative measures of recovery which may be available. Two of these have already been discussed. [See § 1.5(d) supra]. The third measure is that of reliance damages. When expectation damages cannot be approximated with "reasonable certainty," an award of reliance damages serves to foster the policy of judicial convenience by substituting a workable for an unworkable measure of recovery.

EXAMPLE 1. Manufacturer enters into a contract with shipper to have a product shipped to a convention for display. His expectation is not that the display will result in immediate sales but rather that it will attract interest in his product culminating in eventual sales and also good will for his company. Shipper, who is aware of manufacturer's purpose, breaches the contract by losing the product in transit. Manufacturer's expectation damages cannot be measured with "reasonable certainty" since it is not known whether the display would have resulted in future sales or good will. A more workable measure of recovery would be manufacturer's reliance expenses. These would include, but not be limited to, the amount which he paid for the rental of exhibition space and the amount which it cost him to send his employees to the convention.

EXAMPLE 2. In the oft-cited case of *Chicago Coliseum Club v. Dempsey*, 265 Ill.App. 542 (1932) a promoter entered into a contract with well-known boxer, Jack Dempsey, in which Dempsey agreed to engage in a match to determine the heavyweight championship of the world. After a breach by Dempsey and subsequent suit by the promoter, the court held that promoter's loss of potential profits was too speculative to be recoverable as damages. However, promoter was permitted to recover those expenses which he incurred in reliance on his belief that Dempsey would perform the contract. These included payments made to an architect for plans for a stadium in which the match was to be held, reasonable expenses of an employee who traveled to Colorado for the purpose of having Dempsey take a physical examination for insurance, and expenses incurred in making arrangements with a railroad for publicity and special trains and accomodations.

(b) Cases of Impossibility of Performance or Frustration of Purpose

When a contract has become impossible to perform, or when its purpose has been totally frustrated, the parties are usually relieved from liability for future performance; hence neither party will be able to obtain expectation damages from the other. However, if one party has conferred benefits on the other prior to the occurrence of the supervening event which renders performance impossible, most courts will decree that the party receiving the benefits must make restitution to the party conferring them. The difficult case arises when a party has incurred reliance expenses prior to the supervening event but those expenditures have not conferred anything of value on the defendant. The case law does not *expressly* recognize reliance damages as an appropriate measure of recovery in such cases. Yet, when one examines the "impossibility" cases in which the courts have awarded "restitution," one discovers that in many of them the courts are actually awarding reliance damages, as no actual benefits have been conferred on the defendant.

EXAMPLE. Plaintiff contracts to move a large building belonging to the defendant from a lot on

Third Street to a lot on First Street. After the building has been moved about half the distance to the lot on First Street, it is destroyed by fire, through no fault of plaintiff's. Both parties are excused from further performance because the supervening event has rendered performance impossible. For the same reason, plaintiff cannot maintain a successful suit for expectation damages. In one similar case, however, plaintiff was allowed restitution for the reasonable value of his services even though services did not result in any tangible benefit to defendant. Discussing this and similar cases, one leading commentator has noted that "we find much reason to suspect that in some of [these cases] the reliance interest has received protection under [the] alias [of restitution]. There is exemplified in these cases the same attenuation of the requirement of benefit [that we find] . . . in connection with contracts falling within the Statute of Frauds." [See Subsection (c) infra].

(c) Contracts Within the Statute of Frauds

Because an oral contract which is unenforceable under the statute of frauds is neither illegal nor against public policy, it is well-settled that a plaintiff who has conferred benefits upon a defendant who then refuses to perform may obtain restitution of those benefits. See § 2.4(b) supra. It is equally clear, however, that the statute does preclude any recovery of expectation damages. The difficult question is whether reliance damages —plaintiff's expenditures which have conferred no tangible benefits on defendant—are recoverable. Until recently, a majority of courts held that to grant reimbursement for reliance expenses would violate the statute; thus, reimbursement was denied. A minority, however, were willing to grant relief either under a "restitution" theory (with an attenuation of the requirement of "benefit") or under the theory that the promisee's foreseeable reliance estops the promisor from asserting the statute of frauds.

EXAMPLE. Farmer orally contracts with Owner to manage Owner's farm in Texas for one year in return for a percentage of the crops raised. The one year period is to start when Farmer arrives in Texas. In reliance on the contract, Farmer sells his home in Kentucky and at considerable expense moves his family and belongings to Texas. As soon as Farmer arrives, Owner repudiates. The oral contract is unenforceable because it is within the "one year" provision of the statute of frauds. Farmer sues. Until recently, in a majority of jurisdictions, Farmer's moving expenses were not recoverable because those reliance costs did not provide any benefit to Owner. Today, however, some courts allow restitutionary recovery of such costs because they were incurred at the request of Owner and hence conferred a "benefit" (albeit intangible) on him. Other courts grant recovery on the theory that Farmer's foreseeable reliance estops Owner from asserting the statute of frauds.

Restatement Position—Reliance Renders Oral Contract Enforceable

§ 139 of the Restatement of Contracts 2d, which is entitled "Enforcement by Virtue of Action in Reliance," provides: "A promise which the promisor should reasonably expect to induce action or forbearance on the part of the promisee or a third person and which does induce the action or forbearance is enforceable notwithstanding the Statute of Frauds if injustice can be avoided only by enforcement of the promise. The remedy granted for breach is to be limited as justice requires." Moreover, "in some cases it may be appropriate to measure relief by the extent of the promisee's reliance rather than by the terms of the promise." Restatement 2d, § 139, Comment 1. The effect of this Restatement provision is that reasonable reliance renders the contract enforceable. The court, however, has discretion as to the measure of relief and may award either the full expectation or otherwise merely compensation for reliance expenditures—whichever "justice requires." Thus, in the immediately preceding example, the court has discretion either to award Farmer his full loss of bargain (i.e., the value of the crops which were promised to him) or otherwise simply to compensate him for his moving expenses and other related costs.

(d) *Donative Promises Reasonably Inducing Action or Forbearance—Promissory Estoppel Under Restatement 2d, § 90*

Under § 90 of the Restatement 2d of Contracts, a donative promise which reasonably induces action or forbearance "is binding if injustice can be avoided only by enforcement of the promise." The situation contemplated by this provision is that of a donative promise which is detrimentally relied upon by the promisee or a third person. In such cases, the promise, even though not supported by consideration, is enforceable, but "the remedy granted for breach may be limited as justice requires." Restatement 2d, § 90(1). Because reliance is the main basis for enforcement of this non-bargain, "relief may sometimes be   .   .   . measured by the extent of the promisee's reliance rather than by the terms of the promise." Restatement 2d of Contracts, § 90, Comment d. Imposition of such a limitation on remedy is within the court's discretion, to be exercised as "justice requires."

EXAMPLE. Uncle, knowing that his poverty-stricken Nephew is contemplating the possibility of enrolling in law school, promises Nephew that he will give him a gift of $10,000 on his 25th birthday. In reliance on Uncle's promise, Nephew enrolls in law school and borrows $6,000 for tuition, books and other expenses. One week prior to Nephew's 25th birthday, Uncle notifies Nephew of his intention to revoke the promise. Uncle's promise is binding even though it was not supported by consideration. The court can, in an exercise of its discretion, order full scale enforcement of the entire promise, i.e., enter a damage award of $10,000. However, because there has been no "bargain" between Uncle and Nephew, the court may believe that justice does not require an award of expectation damages. Instead, it may choose to compensate Nephew for the injury to his reliance interest by ordering Uncle to pay reliance damages, or $6,000.

§ 3.2 Reliance and Expectation as Mutually Exclusive Measures of Recovery

Because reliance damages represent costs which the aggrieved party would have incurred even if the other party had fully performed the contract, an award of reliance damages along with an award of expectation damages would place the aggrieved party in a better position than he would have been in had there been no breach. To allow such a recovery would be to allow plaintiff to recover twice for the same wrong. Thus, reliance damages and expectation damages are mutually exclusive remedies. They may not be recovered cumulatively.

EXAMPLE. Seller and buyer enter into a contract for the sale of four machines designed to recondition old rubber. The sale price is $12,000.

After buyer spends $15,000 building a foundation for the machines, but before he has paid any part of the purchase price, seller repudiates the agreement and refuses to deliver the machines. Buyer subsequently "covers" (see § 5.2 infra) by purchasing similar machines elsewhere for a reasonable price, $20,000. Buyer will be able to recover his expectation damages, or $8,000 (see § 5.2(a) infra). However, he will not be able to recover in *addition* the $15,000 reliance costs expended in building the foundation as these are costs which he would have incurred even if defendant had fully performed.

§ 3.3 Expectation Interest as Ceiling on Recovery of Reliance Damages

When a person enters into a contract, she ordinarily anticipates that her gains will exceed her expenditures. Thus, in most cases, the expectation interest will exceed the reliance interest. After the contract has been breached, however, hindsight may reveal that the aggrieved party has entered into a losing bargain—that had the contract been performed by defendant, plaintiff's expenditures would have exceeded her gross profits from the transaction. In such cases, the courts will not award full reimbursement of losses in reliance on the contract because to do so would be to put the plaintiff in a better position than she would have occupied had the contract been fully performed.

Instead, the amount of net loss that plaintiff would have suffered will be subtracted from reliance damages, so that recovery shall in no event exceed the amount of the expectation interest. However, the burden is on defendant to prove that plaintiff would have suffered a net loss on the contract and also to prove the amount of that loss.

EXAMPLE. Seller and Buyer enter into a contract for the sale of four machines designed to recondition old rubber. After buyer spends $15,000 building a foundation for the machines, but before she has paid any part of the purchase price, seller repudiates the agreement and refuses to deliver. Buyer is unable to purchase similar machines elsewhere. Claiming that her expectation cannot be estimated with reasonable certainty, buyer brings suit seeking reimbursement for her $15,000 reliances expenditures. At trial, *seller* introduces evidence that the purchase price of the machines was $20,000 and that buyer's proceeds from the use of the machines would have been only $25,000. Thus, argues seller, buyer would have suffered a net loss of $10,000 on the contract (i.e. $20,000 purchase price plus $15,000 reliance costs offset by proceeds of only $25,000 equals a net loss of $10,000). If *defendant* (seller) can prove the amount of this net loss with reasonable certainty, it will be deducted from buyer's reliance damages, and buyer will recover only $5,000. This $5,000 is, of course, the same amount as his loss of bargain (i.e. he would have paid seller $20,000 for a machine that yielded proceeds of $25,000). Thus, in suits for reliance damages, the expectation interest, if provable, represents a ceiling on the amount which can be recovered.

CHAPTER 4

SPECIFIC PERFORMANCE

Specific performance is an equitable remedy which attempts to give the injured party the "benefit of his bargain" by compelling the breaching party to actually render the performance agreed upon. It is often referred to as the "most perfect" form of relief available, in that it gives the injured party the very thing he bargained for rather than seeking to quantify that party's damages and to provide compensation in "mere" money. A decree of specific performance is enforced through the contempt powers of the court.

§ 4.1 Specific Performance Dependent on the Inadequacy of Money Damages

Historically, equitable relief was intended to be "supplementary" in nature. Thus, equitable jurisdiction could be had over a particular dispute only upon a showing that the remedies available at law (i. e. money damages) were inadequate to provide full and complete compensation to the plaintiff. This requirement still exists, and specific performance will not be decreed if money damages will adequately redress the losses which were caused by defendant's breach.

When a judge decides whether or not money damages are adequate to provide full and adequate compensation, she is, in large part, addressing a factual question which turns on the circumstances of the case at hand. Such a decision cannot be made on the basis of a set of black-letter principles. However, some of the more frequently mentioned criteria for determining the inadequacy of legal relief are:

(1) The inability of money to "buy" a duplicate or substantial equivalent of the promised performance (subsection (a) infra);

(2) The difficulty or impossibility of estimating damages with "reasonable certainty" (subsection (b) infra);

(3) The existing or prospective insolvency of the defendant (subsection (c) infra) and;

(4) The probability that full compensation cannot be had without multiple litigation (subsection (d) infra).

(a) The Inability of Money, Awarded as Damages, to "Buy" a Duplicate or Substantial Equivalent of the Performance Promised by the Defendant

In most cases an award of money damages will give plaintiff the benefit of his bargain by enabling him to secure the equivalent of the defendant's promised performance from a third party. Thus, when defendant's breach consists of a failure to deliver goods for which there is an existing market, the damage remedy will usually be considered adequate.   However, when the subject of the transaction is rare or unique, or cannot be obtained at a reasonable price without excessive inconvenience or difficulty, a decree of specific performance will often be necessary in order to effect complete justice.

EXAMPLE 1.   A contracts to sell to B 1000 bushels of wheat at a price of $4.00 per bushel. On the date set for delivery, A repudiates.   Assuming that there exists an established market where B can purchase wheat of a similar nature and quality, money damages representing B's lost expectation (See Chapter 5) will be adequate to do full and complete justice.   A suit by B for specific performance will fail.

EXAMPLE 2.   A contracts to sell B "The Nude" by Picasso for $250,000.   If A breaches the contract, a suit for specific performance by B should be successful as B's damage remedy is clearly inadequate.   B's expectation was to obtain the specific painting and no amount of money awarded as damages will allow him to enter the market place and fulfill that expectation.   See UCC 2–716 (discussed in Chapter 5).

Contracts for the Sale of Land: Vendee's Right to Specific Performance

The aggrieved vendee under a contract for the sale of land will generally be entitled to specific performance.   The law presumes that each parcel of land is a unique entity and that damages will therefore be inadequate as a remedy for breach. The application of this rule does not depend on the land being unique in fact;   it need not have any especially desirable qualities, such as advantageous location or fertility.   Rather, the rule stems from the historical concern with ownership of real property which is still embodied in many aspects of Anglo-American law.   Thus, many courts have stated that "specific performance of a contract to convey land is merely a matter of course."

EXAMPLE.   Buyer contracts with vendor to purchase Blackacre (a frequently sold piece or rural real estate) for a price of $750,000.   Vendor repudiates the contract and argues that because an adjacent farm of substantially equivalent size and fertility is for sale at a reasonable price, an award of damages to Buyer would be a fully adequate remedy.   The argument will fail.   Buyer is entitled to specific performance despite her ability to obtain a substantially equivalent parcel of land elsewhere.

Contracts for the Sale of Land: Vendor's Right to Specific Performance

An aggrieved vendor of land will generally be entitled to a decree of specific performance when the purchaser repudiates the contract prior to conveyance of title.   Such a decree will require the purchaser to accept title and to pay the purchase price in full. Two reasons are frequently advanced to justify this result. First, it is argued, damages measured by the market price-contract price differential are not adequate for a vendor who has a need for money. Land is not a liquid asset; it is often difficult to sell. Even if market value can be established, a purchaser may not be available. In such a case, if specific performance is not allowed, the aggrieved vendor will be "stuck" with his land and a damage award which might be very small in proportion to the total purchase price. This rationale is not particularly convincing; for, specific performance is a remedy which is available not only to vendors who can demonstrate difficulty in re-selling the land but also to those who could re-sell with ease. If difficulty of resale is truly the reason for the willingness of the courts to decree specific performance, then query why the courts do not require the aggrieved vendor to establish that he has made "a reasonable effort to resell [the land] at a reasonable price or [that] the circumstances reasonably indicate that such effort will be unavailing." Cf. UCC 2–709(1)(b) (discussed in Chapter 7).

The second reason for granting specific performance to an aggrieved vendor is the concept of "mutuality of remedies." Because the *vendee* would be entitled to specific performance upon the vendor's default, many courts have stated that the concept of "mutuality" requires that the vendor be given a reciprocal right. The "mutuality of remedies" doctrine, however, has been discredited, and is of little force today. (See § 4.2(c) infra).

Contracts for the Sale of Goods

An aggrieved *buyer's* right to specific performance for breach of a contract for the sale of goods is controlled by UCC 2–716. This provision is discussed in Chapter 5. When the *seller* is the aggrieved party, his right to specific relief is controlled by UCC 2–709 ("Action for the Price") which is discussed in Chapter 7.

(b) The Difficulty or Impossibility of Estimating Damages with Reasonable Certainty

A second factor which can militate in favor of a decree of specific performance is the inability of the court to make a reasonable estimate of plaintiff's damages. As a prerequisite to any damage recovery, the plaintiff must demonstrate with "reasonable certainty" the amount of harm he has suffered as a result of defendant's breach. See § 1.5 supra. Often, this is not possible; for example, the object of the contract may have no market value, or the full effects of the defendant's breach may not be known or knowable. In these cases, limiting the plaintiff to a damage remedy might result in the total denial of relief. In cases where such a result would be unjust, specific performance might be allowed.

EXAMPLE. Owner promises to pay a sum of money to Railroad in consideration for Railroad's promise to build and maintain a spur track and depot on Owner's land. In reliance on his contract with Railroad, Owner constructs a large, expensive hotel to accommodate tourists who will be arriving on Railroad's trains. Railroad subsequently breaches the contract by deciding to build the spur track and depot twenty miles away from Owner's property. It is likely that Owner has been damaged. Railroad's breach will probably depreciate the value of Owner's hotel by increasing the cost of transportation which will be required to and from the depot and decreasing the number of people who will stay at the hotel. However, the harm is of such a nature that the amount of damages could not be assessed with any reasonable degree of certainty. Thus, absent other relevant factors, a court might be willing to grant a decree of specific performance.

Existence of Sentimental or Other Non-Monetary Value

If the object of a particular transaction has sentimental or other non-monetary value to the plaintiff, a damage award, which will enable plaintiff to purchase a physical equivalent, could defeat the purpose of the transaction. In such cases, specific performance may be decreed.

EXAMPLE. Plaintiff contracts to purchase the old grandfather clock which for 50 years had stood in the hallway of his boyhood home and for which he had developed great sentimental attachment. Upon defendant's breach, plaintiff may properly be granted specific performance. Even though an identical clock made by the same manufacturer can easily be purchased in the market place, a damage award would not adequately compensate plaintiff because, under the rules relating to recovery of expectation damages, losses based on the subjective or non-monetary value of the subject matter are generally not compensable (See § 1.1(b) supra).

(c) Defendant's Insolvency as Affecting the Inadequacy of Damages

The existing or prospective insolvency of the defendant may indicate that an award of money damages will not fully compensate plaintiff for his injury. Recovery of a damage award against a "judgment proof" defendant can often be a hollow victory; in such cases, an award of specific performance may be appropriate. However, a decree of specific performance against an insolvent defendant might, in some instances, conflict with applicable bankruptcy legislation which generally prohibits distribution of the estate of an insolvent debtor in a manner which would operate as a preference of one creditor over others in the same class. In the event of such a conflict with the interests of other creditors, plaintiff will not be granted specific performance unless he can establish his right to it under some express statutory provision.

EXAMPLE. Seller and Buyer contract for the sale by Seller to Buyer of industrial machinery for $10,000. Under the terms of the contract, Buyer is to pay $2,000 in advance of delivery and the remaining $8,000 in four monthly installments after receipt of the goods. Buyer makes the initial $2,000 payment; four days after receiving that payment, Seller declares bankruptcy. Under UCC 2–502, Buyer may recover the goods. See § 5.6(c) infra. According to that statutory provision, if the buyer has paid part or all of the price and the seller has become insolvent within ten days after receipt of the first installment of the payment, the buyer may recover the goods by tendering the balance due. This is, of course, a form of specific performance. The purpose of the ten-day limitation is to protect the rights of other creditors of the insolvent seller. In balancing the rights of the buyer and the seller's other creditors, the Code gives a preference to the buyer for a very brief period of time because an imminently insolvent seller who accepts part of the price will usually know that he will not be able to perform his side of the bargain. By accepting Buyer's money under such circumstances, Seller is acting in a manner that is close to being fraudulent.

(d) Prevention of a Multiplicity of Suits

If it appears that full compensation "at law" would require a multiplicity of suits, involving either third parties or repeated actions against the defendant, the legal remedy may be considered inadequate and specific performance decreed.

EXAMPLE. A enters into a contract of insurance with Company X, which provides that upon A's "total and permanent" disability he shall receive benefits of $100 per month for life. A subsequently files a claim under the policy, but Company X refuses to recognize the disability. A then institutes suit to collect his benefits. In the ensuing litigation, Company X argues that A's disability is only temporary and suggests that any claim filed by A subsequent to the lawsuit will be contested. If the court finds that A's disability is, in fact, permanent, a decree of specific performance might be appropriate. Because it appears likely that Company X will refuse to perform in the future, a damage award (based solely on Company X's previous non-payments) might necessitate multiple litigation by A against Company X. The court can prevent such potential litigation by ordering Company X to specifically perform its contract with A.

§ 4.2 Specific Performance as a Discretionary Remedy

Even if the plaintiff can establish that his legal remedies are inadequate, specific performance will not be granted automatically. It is a well established maxim that specific performance is not a matter of absolute right to either party; it is a matter which rests with the discretion of the court. This maxim does not imply that judicial discretion is unfettered; the granting of denial of specific performance must be based on sound reasons, and a decision made arbitrarily will be reversed on appeal. Rather, the maxim indicates that a court should look to the potential effects of a decree of specific performance and may justify its refusal to grant such relief on a number of grounds which would not serve as defenses in an action for damages. These include: the degree of judicial supervision which specific performance would require (subsection (a)), the potentially harsh or inequitable results of specific enforcement (subsection (b)), and the inability of the court to guarantee the reciprocal performance of the plaintiff (subsection (c)).

(a) Degree of Judicial Supervision

Judicial resources are limited, and where the difficulty of supervising a decree of specific performance would be disproportionate to the benefit the decree would confer upon the plaintiff, equitable relief may be denied. For this reason, specific performance is frequently denied if the contract requires the application of the skill and expertise of the defendant or involves a lengthy performance which would require continuing supervision by the court.

Construction Contracts

Historically, contracts to build or repair were not specifically enforced. This principle was based, in part, on the fact that money damages would usually enable plaintiff to obtain an adequate substitute performance. However, when denying specific performance, courts also stressed the difficulties of long-term supervision of a decree which orders a defendant to build or repair something. While this traditional view is still followed in a number of jurisdictions, many commentators and a growing number of courts now believe that the difficulties of enforcing a construction contract have been overstated. The modern trend is towards a greater liberality in decreeing specific performance of such contracts if the damage remedy is inadequate.

EXAMPLE. Same facts as in a previous Example. Owner promises to pay a sum of money to Railroad in consideration for Railroad's promise to build and maintain a spur track and depot on Owner's land. In reliance on his contract with Railroad, Owner constructs a large, expensive hotel to accommodate tourists who will be arriving on Railroad's trains. Railroad subsequently breaches the contract by deciding to build the spur track and depot twenty miles away from Owner's property. As noted in the previous example, Owner has been damaged, but the harm is of such a nature that the amount of damages cannot be assessed with any reasonable degree of certainty. This factor may make the case an appropriate one for specific performance. Nevertheless, under the traditional doctrine, because the contract calls for a continuity of acts on the part of Railroad, which supposedly would require the constant attention of the court in securing enforcement of its decree, specific performance would not have been granted. Several recent cases, however, have allowed specific relief in such instances.

Personal Service Contracts

Generally, in the absence of obligations arising under labor or civil rights statutes, a court of equity will not order a defaulting employer or employee to specifically perform a personal service contract. A breach of such a contract inevitably results in or from a breakdown in the relationship between the parties, and a court decree cannot reinstate good feelings and/or a desire to work. An additional reason for the reluctance to grant specific performance against a defaulting employee is that such a decree is considered oppressive and suggestive of involuntary servitude.

Non-Competition Covenants

While the courts will usually not order a default-ing employee to specifically perform the *af-firmative* duty imposed by a personal service con-tract, a promise by the employee not to compete with the employer will often be specifically en-forced through a decree which restrains the em-ployee from opening a competing operation or working for plaintiff's competitors. Because spe-cific enforcement of a non-competition covenant does not compel defendant to *do* anything (but only to refrain from doing something) such a decree requires very little judicial supervision. However, enforcement of non-competition clauses will be granted only where the time period, geo-graphical location, and other provisions contained in the clause are reasonably designed to protect the employer from an actual harm, and where the ability of the defendant to earn a living will not be unjustly impaired.

EXAMPLE. Singer enters into a one year con-tract for an exclusive engagement at Owner's thea-ter. The contract contains a clause which pro-hibits Singer from appearing at any other compet-ing establishment in the same city during the one year life of the contract. Two months later, Sing-er receives a more lucrative offer from the compet-ing theater across the street and repudiates the contract with Owner. It is very unlikely that a court would enter a decree compelling Singer to perform at Owner's theater. However, the court might restrain Singer from performing at the competing theater but only if necessary to prevent actual damage to Owner's business.

(b) Potentially Harsh or Inequitable Results

It is within the discretion of the court to refuse equitable relief if it is shown that specific enforcement of a contract might produce harsh, inequitable, oppressive, or unconscionable results. When such a potential exists, the judge is given wide discretionary latitude, and what shocks the conscience of one court may be deemed to be acceptable by another. The factors discussed below are not all-inclusive but do represent some of the considerations commonly taken into account when deciding whether specific performance will produce harsh or inequitable results.

Supervening Events Not Within the Contemplation of the Parties

Specific performance may properly be denied where the granting of the decree would work hardship or injustice on the defendant because of supervening events which were not within the contemplation of the parties when the contract was formed. The court may refuse equitable relief even if the supervening event is not of a magnitude which would relieve defendant of liability in an action for damages.

EXAMPLE. Businessman contracts to purchase a parcel of land from Owner for the purpose of establishing a warehouse storage facility. Between the time the contract is signed and the time set for delivery of the deed, the city council re-zones the land for residential purposes only. Businessman refuses to complete the transaction and repudiates the contract. The courts of the jurisdiction have repeatedly held that an intervening zoning change does not discharge the duties of a purchaser in a contract for the sale of land. Therefore a suit by Owner for damages arising from Businessman's repudiation would be successful. However, a suit for specific performance might possibly fail as a judge might deem it harsh to force businessman to accept title to land which is now useless to him.

The "Clean Hands" Doctrine

It is often stated that the plaintiff in a suit for equitable relief must come into court with "clean hands." Thus, specific performance may be denied when plaintiff's practices are "unclean" even though not sufficiently wrongful either to discharge defendant from liability or to deny plaintiff damages. In an early case, the U.S. Supreme Court stated that "a court of equity acts only when and as conscience commands, and if the conduct of the plaintiff be offensive to the dictates of natural justice; then, whatever rights he possesses and whatever use he may make of them in a court of law, he will be held remediless in a court of equity."

EXAMPLE. Football Team enters into a three year contract with Player, a current college football star. The contract is not illegal; however, it is made in violation of college athletic rules which render a player ineligible for a college team as soon as he signs with a professional team. To circumvent this restriction, Player and the Football Team agree to keep the contract secret until the end of the college season. At the end of the college season, Team repudiates the contract and Player sues for specific performance. While the circumstances surrounding the agreement might not suffice to discharge Team from its contractual responsibility to Player, a decree of specific performance might properly be denied under the "clean hands" doctrine as the transaction is tainted with unethical behavior.

Laches (Delay)

Specific performance will be denied if the plaintiff has unreasonably delayed in seeking equitable relief even if the statute of limitations has not tolled. There is no concrete rule as to the particular length or form of the delay; the defense of "laches" becomes available if the court finds that the delay was unreasonable and that (because of the delay) specific performance will result in hardship.

EXAMPLE. Vendor breaches a contract to convey certain land to purchaser by not removing certain encumberances from the title as required by the contract. Vendor subsequently clears the cloud on title, and conveys this fact to purchaser. Purchaser, however, takes no action to enforce his contractual rights until two years after learning that title has been cleared. By that time, vendor, believing that purchaser is no longer interested in the land, constructs a residence for his family on it. Purchaser than sues for specific performance. Vendor could successfully use the defense of "laches" against purchaser, even if the statute of limitations has not run out.

Adverse Effect on Public Interest

Equity will take into account the effect its decision might have on the public interest and may grant or deny specific performance accordingly. While a contract which is illegal or against public policy will not be enforced at law, the scope of the interests considered by a court of equity is much broader and is not limited to those circumstances which would provide a defense to an action for damages.

EXAMPLE. A agrees to lease to B a building in a shopping center which is in very close proximity to a residential area. At the time of the contract, A is unaware of the fact that B intends to use the building for the operation of a "massage parlor" which is neither illegal nor in violation of local zoning regulations. When the intended use becomes known, the nearby residents become outraged. Ninety percent of those residents sign a petition threatening that if A leases the building to B, they (the residents) will not patronize other businesses owned by A. A subsequently repudiates the contract, and B sues for specific performance. If the court finds that the potential disadvantage to the community as well as to A is great, it can refuse specific performance on grounds of public policy, even though A might be liable in damages for breach of contract.

(c) Requirement That the Reciprocal Performance of the Plaintiff be Secured to the Satisfaction of the Court

Before a court will order a defendant to specifically perform his contract, it must be satisfied that the reciprocal performance promised by the plaintiff will, in fact, be tendered. The court has power to require plaintiff to give adequate security to this effect. The potential lack of return performance by plaintiff presents no problem in an action for damages, because the expectation damages formula (§ 1.1(a) supra) subtracts the cost of any part performance not yet rendered by the plaintiff (the "costs avoided") from her recovery. In a suit for specific performance, however, it is, of course, impossible to make any such deduction for plaintiff's non-performance. It is thus quite possible that a court could compel the defendant to specifically perform, and that plaintiff could subsequently refuse to tender the agreed upon exchange performance—a result made no less likely by the hostilities inevitably generated by litigation. Thus, in framing its decree, the court can include terms which will secure the plaintiffs return performance, and if it proves impossible or impracticable to adequately secure that reciprocal performance, specific performance can be denied.

EXAMPLE 1. Plaintiff contracts with City X for the city to extend its water and sewer lines to plaintiff's new housing development for a fee of $50,000 to be paid upon completion of the work. City X repudiates the contract after the housing development is partially completed, and Plaintiff sues for specific performance. If the court finds a decree of specific performance appropriate, the decree may properly be made conditional upon plaintiff providing adequate security that she will perform her part of the exchange (the payment of $50,000). Such security could be easily arranged by requiring payment in installments as the work progresses (rather than on completion), by requiring plaintiff to execute a bond, or by requiring that the money be deposited with the court pending completion of the defendant's performance.

EXAMPLE 2. Under an employment contract between Miner and Engineer, Engineer agrees to provide his expertise and skill in mine shaft construction in consideration of Miner's promise to convey a plot of valuable mineral-bearing land to him after one year's service. Miner wrongfully breaches the contract. Engineer sues for specific performance, requesting a transfer of the land. Specific performance will probably be denied. There is no way in which the court can adequately secure Engineer's promised performance, as a court will usually not specifically enforce a personal service contract. (See subsection (a) supra). Thus, Engineer will be limited to his damage remedy. However if Miner breaches after Engineer has performed all the agreed-upon services, a decree of specific performance will be granted.

Doctrine of "Mutuality of Remedy" Discredited

A number of older cases have purported to base the decision to grant or deny specific performance on a doctrine of "mutuality of remedies." There were two parts to that doctrine: (1) If the defendant in a contract suit would have been allowed specific performance, if he were the injured party, the plaintiff will be allowed specific performance; and (2) if the defendant would not have been entitled to specific performance if he were the injured party, the plaintiff will be denied specific performance as well. The purpose of the first part of the doctrine was to do justice between the parties under the maxim "Equality is Equity."

The purpose of the second part was to guarantee that the defendant, having been compelled to perform, could then compel plaintiff to render his part of the bargained-for exchange. Both parts of the doctrine have been discredited and are of little force today. Part (1) seems to have been based solely on an aphorism, not buttressed by any rationale. Although the rationale behind part (2) is commendable, it can be achieved through the previously discussed methods of requiring that the plaintiff's reciprocal performance be secured to the satisfaction of the court.

§ 4.3 Specific Performance Plus Damages

Specific performance and money damages are not mutually exclusive remedies, and a court possesses the discretion to award both where necessary to provide full compensation to the injured party. This will frequently be the case where the defendant's breach has resulted in interim consequential damages (EXAMPLE 1), or where *part* of the defendant's performance would be difficult or impossible to compel through a decree of specific performance (EXAMPLES 2 and 3). Of course, in framing a decree granting both specific performance and damages, care must be taken to avoid providing double compensation for a single injury.

EXAMPLE 1. Vendor and Purchaser enter into a contract for the sale of a building which

Purchaser intends to lease to X Company for $1,000 per month. Vendor is to deliver the deed on May 1; Purchaser's lease agreement with X Company begins on the same date. On May 1, Vendor repudiates the agreement. Purchaser sues for specific performance which is granted on June 1. Because Vendor's breach has resulted in an interim consequential to loss to Purchaser of one month's rent under his lease agreement with X, the court will also award money damages to compensate for that loss.

EXAMPLE 2. Buyer agrees to convey two parcels of land to Developer. In return, Developer promises to convey one parcel of land to Buyer and to construct on it a 6,000 square foot structure suitable for use as an office building. Developer repudiates the entire contract, and Buyer sues for specific performance. Even if the court refuses to order Developer to specifically perform his promise to construct the building (See § 4.2(a) supra), it might still order conveyance of the promised parcel of land and award damages representing the cost of constructing the building.

EXAMPLE 3. Buyer enters into an agreement with Seller for the conveyance of real property, the title of which is to be "clear" and free of encumbrances. Upon conducting the title search, Buyer discovers that the title is not "clear" and that Seller does not have title to the mineral rights underlying the land—a material breach of contract. Even though Seller is incapable of performing as contracted, Buyer may still elect to seek specific performance of the contract with an abatement in price representing the dimunition of the value of the land caused by the title defect.

§ 4.4 Indirect Specific Enforcement of Affirmative Contractual Promises Through Direct Enforcement of Negative Obligations

Affirmative contractual promises are often accompanied by expressed or implied negative duties to forbear from actions inconsistent with the purpose of the contract. For example, a promise to sell a chattel to the plaintiff contains an implied promise not to sell it to a third party. A promise to market only the plaintiff's product contains an implied promise to forbear from marketing a competitor's. Decrees of specific performance requiring affirmative action are sometimes denied because of the difficulties of judicial supervision (§ 4.2(a) supra). However, a court of equity in framing its decree, may be able to encourage performance of the affirmative obligation, while avoiding the difficulties of supervision, simply by enjoining the accompanying negative obligation. (Example 1 infra). Such indirect enforcement will not be attempted if specific enforcement of the affirmative duty would have been denied for policy reasons rather than because of the difficulties of enforcement or supervision (Example 2 infra).

EXAMPLE 1. The XYZ Canning Company enters into a contract with Grower whereby Grower agrees to plant his entire acreage with loganberries and sell the entire crop to XYZ at the end of the year for a predetermined price. Midway through the planting season, the great loganberry blight ravages the countryside, and prices skyrocket. Grower's acreage is not affected by the blight. Grower repudiates the contract with XYZ and signs with another company for a higher price. XYZ sues for specific performance. Enforcement of the affirmative duty to grow and harvest the crop might entail an inordinate amount of judicial supervision; thus specific performance might be denied. However, if legal remedies are inadequate, XYZ might be entitled to an injunction which restrains Grower from selling his crop to any other company. Grower may still decide to let his land lie fallow, or decide not to harvest or sell any berries already planted. But any loganberries sold must be sold to XYZ, and Grower's self-interest will make it likely that he will fulfill his contractual obligations.

EXAMPLE 2. Farmer hires Laborer under a contract with a one year duration. After two months, severe acrimony develops between the parties. Upon Laborer's repudiation of the contract, Farmer seeks an injunction prohibiting Laborer from working for "any other person" for the remaining life of the contract. While such an injunction might well be effective in enforcing laborer's affirmative contractual duties to Farmer, the decree will probably be denied. One of the reasons for the denial of specific performance of personal service contracts is that such enforcement is suggestive of involuntary servitude. (See § 4.2(a) supra). Equity will not attempt to do indirectly that which it refuses, for policy reasons, to accomplish directly. While non-competition clauses may be enforced under certain circumstances (see § 4.2(a) supra) the purpose of such enforcement is to protect the plaintiff from actual harm, not to compel the defendant's performance by impairing his ability to earn a living elsewhere. In the instant case, it is unlikely that an injunction is necessary to prevent actual harm to Farmer's business. The injunction which he seeks would restrain Laborer from working for "any other person" not merely for persons in competition with Farmer. Moreover, because Laborer's services are not extraordinary or unique, any harm to Farmer can be remedied by obtaining a substitute employee, and suing Laborer for any damages which have resulted from his breach.

PART II

CONTRACTS FOR THE SALE OF GOODS: BUYER'S AND SELLERS' REMEDIES UNDER ARTICLE II OF THE UNIFORM COMMERCIAL CODE.

INTRODUCTION

When a contract for the sale of goods has been breached, the range of remedies available to the aggrieved party will be governed by Article 2 of the Uniform Commercial Code (UCC). Under the remedial framework of Article 2, the scope of remedies available to the aggrieved party will always depend on whether or not the buyer has accepted the goods. This is true regardless of whether the aggrieved party is the buyer or seller. Therefore, Part II of this Nutshell, which describes and analyzes the statutory remedies available to aggrieved buyers and sellers, has been divided into four chapters: Chapter 5: Remedies Available to Buyer When He Has Not Accepted the Goods; Chapter 6: Remedies Available to Buyer After He Has Accepted the Goods, Including Remedies For Breach of Warranty; Chapter 7: Remedies Available to Seller When Buyer Defaults and Has Not Accepted the Goods; and Chapter 8: Remedies Available to Seller When Buyer Defaults After Accepting the Goods.

In addition, it should be noted that the sales contract itself may attempt to control the remedies available to seller or buyer. This can be accomplished either through a liquidated damages clause (UCC 2–718) or through a contractual modification or limitation of remedy (UCC 2–719). These topics are explored in Chapters Nine and Ten.

CHAPTER 5

REMEDIES AVAILABLE TO BUYER WHEN HE HAS NOT ACCEPTED THE GOODS

UCC 2–711, which lists the remedies available to a buyer where the seller fails to make delivery or repudiates, or the buyer rightfully rejects, provides that the buyer may *cancel* and may, *in addition to recovering so much of the price as has been paid*, choose between cover (UCC 2–712) and damages for non-delivery (UCC 2–713). A third choice, available only "in proper case[s]" is specific performance or replevin (UCC 2–716).

§ 5.1 Cancellation

Cancellation occurs when the buyer puts an end to the contract because of seller's breach. When the buyer cancels, he is allowed to recover any part of the price paid. In addition, he "retains any remedy for breach of the whole contract or any unperformed balance." UCC 2–106(4).

(a) Election of Remedies Not Required

The remedial format set forth in UCC 2–711 is an explicit rejection of the "election of remedies" doctrine. Cancellation of the contract is a form of recission; and, of course "recovering so much of the price as has been paid" is tantamount to obtaining restitution. However, in addition to recission and restitution, buyer is entitled to *expectation* damages under UCC 2–712 (if he covers) or UCC 2–713 (if he does not cover).

§ 5.2   Cover, UCC 2–712

Cover is the act of procuring from others, goods in substitution of those due from the defaulting seller.

(a) Measure of Damages

When the buyer properly covers, he is entitled to recover damages from the seller amounting to the difference between the cost of cover and the contract price plus any incidental or consequential damages (UCC 2–715), (§§ 5.4 and 5.5 infra) but less expenses saved as a result of seller's breach. This damage formula serves two functions. It places the aggrieved buyer in as good a financial position as he would have been in had the contract not been breached, and it enables him to obtain the goods which he needs.

EXAMPLE. Buyer, in New York City, contracts to purchase furniture from a Chicago seller for $50,000. Under the terms of the contract, buyer is to pay the shipping costs of $1,000. Seller repudiates; and buyer, after placing an ad in a trade journal (at a cost of $200) is able to cover in New

York City for $54,000. Under this substitute contract, buyer will pay no shipping or delivery costs. Buyer's total cost of obtaining the furniture under the original contract was $51,000. Under the substitute contract, his total cost is $54,200. Therefore, given the goal of placing the buyer in as good a position as he would have been in had the contract been breached, buyer's recovery should be $3,200. The formula set forth in UCC 2–712 leads to the same result: Cost of cover ($54,000) minus the contract price ($50,000) plus incidental damages ($200 for advertisement) less expenses saved ($1000 in shipping costs). $54,000 − $50,000 + $200 − $1,000 = $3,200.

(b) Manner of Cover

UCC 2–712 allows the aggrieved buyer to "cover" by making a reasonable purchase of goods or a contract to purchase goods in substitution for those due from seller. The buyer must act "in good faith" and "without reasonable delay."

Good Faith

"The test of proper cover is whether at the time and place the buyer acted in good faith and in a reasonable manner, and it is immaterial that hindsight may later prove that the method of cover used was not the cheapest or most effective." UCC 2–712, Official Comment 2. It should be noted that cover is a form of mitigation of damages; and, as is the case under the mitigation doctrine [See § 1.2 supra], the aggrieved party is held to a standard of reasonableness, not perfection.

EXAMPLE. In An Example set forth in § 1.2 (b), seller repudiated a contract for the sale of ore at $15 per ton. Buyer immediately "covered" by purchasing substitute ore at $18 per ton. At the time of seller's breach, there was no established market for ore. At trial, seller was able to prove that had buyer conducted an extensive search, he would have been able to find substitute ore at $17 per ton. Buyer's cover was held to be reasonable and in good faith even though hindsight later proved that the method of cover used was not the cheapest or most effective.

"Without Unreasonable Delay"

The "without unreasonable delay" requirement "is not intended to limit the time necessary for [the aggrieved buyer] to look around and decide as to how he may best effect cover." UCC 2–712, Official Comment 2. Instead, the test under this section is similar to that used in the general provision of the Code regarding reasonable time and seasonable action. That section, UCC 1–204(2), provides that "what is reasonable time for taking any action depends on the nature, purpose, and circumstances of such action."

"Goods in Substitution for Those Due from Seller"

The "goods in substitution for those due from seller" need not be identical to those originally contracted for. "The definition of 'cover' . . . envisages . . . goods not identical with those involved but commercially usable as reasonable substitutes under the circumstances of the particular case and [also] contracts on credit or delivery terms differing from the contract in breach, but again reasonable under the circumstances." UCC 2–712, Official Comment 2. The major problem with the "substitution" requirement is how to determine damages when the cover item is in "substitution for" but of different quality than the item contracted for.

EXAMPLE. In the immediately preceding Example, seller repudiated a contract for the sale of ore at $15 per ton. Buyer immediately covered by purchasing substitute ore at $18 per ton. Suppose this substitute ore was of superior quality to the ore due from seller under the original contract. Clearly, if ore comparable to that contracted for were available, buyer should not be allowed to recover the full difference between his cover price and contract price. But what if the higher quality ore is the only available substitute? Here, the damage award should be consistent with the goal of placing the aggrieved party in as good (but no better) a position as he would have been in had the contract not been breached. Hence, if the superiority of the substitute ore will not benefit the buyer in any way (perhaps he is already under a contract to resell it and cannot raise his price), then buyer should be able to recover the full contract price-cover price differential from seller. On the other hand, if the superior quality of the substitute ore will benefit the buyer (perhaps he can resell it for a higher price than he could have obtained for the ore for which he originally contracted), then the amount of this benefit should be deducted from his recovery.

§ 5.3　Difference Between Contract Price and Market Price, UCC 2–713

After a default by seller, the buyer may choose *not* to cover. In such a case, he is entitled to recover damages based on the difference between the contract price and the prevailing market price at the time he learned of the breach, together with incidental and consequential damages, but less any expenses saved as a result of seller's breach.

(a) Alternative Remedy to UCC 2–712

The remedy provided by UCC 2–712 ("Cover") and the one provided by UCC 2–713 ("Contract-Market Differential") are mutually exclusive. If the aggrieved buyer chooses to purchase substitute goods, his statutory remedy is UCC 2–712. If he chooses not to "cover" (or if he covers unreasonably) his statutory remedy is UCC 2–713. Moreover, the buyer who has chosen to cover cannot ignore UCC 2–712 and sue for the contract-market differential under UCC 2–713 in the event that the latter would yield a larger recovery.

EXAMPLE. S and B enter into a contract for the sale of 1,000 pounds of coffee at $2 per pound, delivery to occur on June 1. On May 1, S notifies B that he has no intention of performing the contract. On that date, the market price for coffee is $3 per pound. B waits until May 28 to cover; and, on that date, he is able to purchase the coffee at $2.25 per pound. B may not ignore UCC 2–712 and sue for the contract-market differential ($1000) under UCC 2–713. UCC 2–713 applies "only when and to the extent that buyer has not covered." UCC 2–713, Official Comment #5. B may recover only the difference between the cost of cover and the contract price, $250.

(b) Exception to Mitigation Doctrine

The remedy provided by UCC 2–713 is a statutory exception to the principle that an aggrieved party must mitigate his damages [See § 1.3 supra]. That is, an aggrieved buyer is under no duty to cover, even if by covering he could have avoided the consequences of the statutory damages imposed by 2–713. However, a buyer who brings suit pursuant to 2–713 is not entitled to recover *conse-*

quential damages [See § 5.5 infra] if those damages could have been "reasonably prevented by cover or otherwise." UCC 2–715(2)(a).

EXAMPLE. On April 1, during a period when the market price for coffee is rapidly fluctuating, S and B contract for the sale of 3000 pounds of coffee at $2 per pound. Payment is to be made when the coffee is delivered, on May 1. At the time of contracting S knows that it is B's intention to resell the coffee, by the cup, at his coffee shop. By April 20, the market price for coffee has climbed to $3 per pound; and, on that date, S notifies B that he is repudiating the contract. By May 1, the market price has fallen to $2.20. Nevertheless, B chooses not to purchase substitute coffee; and, consequently closes his coffee shop for two months. B is entitled to recover $3,000, the difference between the contract price ($6000) and the market price ($9000) at the time when he learned of the breach. This is true even though B could have avoided most of this loss by purchasing substitute coffee on May 1, at $2.20 per pound. If B had mitigated damages by covering on May 1, his damages would have been the difference between the contract price ($6000) and the cover price ($6600) or $600. Because the statutory scheme provided by UCC 2–712 and UCC 2–713 does not impose on B the duty to mitigate by covering, B can recover the entire contract-market differential, $3000. However, since consequential damages can not be recovered if they could reasonably have been prevented by cover, B can not recover the profits which he lost because of closing down his coffee shop.

(c) Exception to Doctrine That Plaintiff Is to Be Put in "As Good a Position as He Would Have Been in"

Another anomalous result of measuring damages pursuant to UCC 2–713 is that that provision will frequently fail to put plaintiff in "as good a position as he would have been in" had the contract not been breached.

EXAMPLE 1. Manufacturer and retailer enter into a contract for the sale of 2000 Star Wars T-shirts at $2 per shirt. Manufacturer breaches; and on that date the market price for those shirts is $2.50. Buyer chooses not to cover; and therefore brings suit pursuant to UCC 2–713, resulting in a recovery of $1000. Assume, however, that if manufacturer had not breached, retailer could have resold the shirts for $4 each, resulting in a $4000 profit. This $4000 lost profit is not recoverable since it could have been prevented by cover. Therefore, measuring damages via 2–713, fails to put plaintiff in as good a position as he would have been in had defendant not breached.

EXAMPLE 2. Same facts except that the reason retailer does not cover is that he realizes that his own market for Star Wars T-shirts is drying

up. Assume that had manufacturer not breached,
retailer would have been forced to sell the shirts at
$1.00 per shirt, or a total loss of $2000. In this
case, damages will still be measured pursuant to
UCC 2–713, and the result will be that buyer will
be put in a better position than he would have
been in had seller performed.

(d) Time and Place for Determining Market Price

Damages based on market price are measured by
the market price at the *time when buyer learns of
the breach* at the *place of tender*. "The general
baseline adopted in this section uses as a yardstick
the market in which the buyer could have obtained
cover had he sought relief. So the place for measuring damages is the place of tender .   .   .
and the crucial time is the time at which the
buyer learns of the breach." UCC 2–713, Official
Comment #1.

Evidence of Market Price at Other Times and Places

"If evidence of a price prevailing at the times or
places described .   .   . [in the immediately preceding paragraph] is not readily available, the
price prevailing within any reasonable time before
or after the time described or in any other place
which in commercial judgment or under usage of
trade would serve as a reasonable substitute for
the one described may be used, making any proper

allowance for the cost of transporting the goods to or from such place." UCC 2-723(2).

Admissibility of Market Quotations

Market quotations published in official publications, trade journals, newspapers, or periodicals of general circulation are admissible in evidence where the prevailing price of goods bought and sold in any established commodity market is in issue. UCC 2-724.

§ 5.4   Incidental Damages, UCC 2-715

In addition to providing a "cover" formula and a "contract-market" formula, both UCC 2-712 and UCC 2-713 provide for the aggrieved buyer's recovery of *incidental* and consequential damages. According to UCC 2-715(1), "Incidental damages resulting from the sellers' breach include expenses reasonably incurred in inspection, receipt, transportation and care and custody of goods rightfully rejected, any commercially reasonable charges, expenses or commissions in connection with effecting cover and any other reasonable expense incident to the delay or other breach." Official Comment #1 lists three typical kinds of incidental damages recoverable under UCC 2-715: (1) damages associated with rightful rejection of goods; [See Chapter 6 for a discussion of rejection]; (2) damages associated with a proper revocation of acceptance [This topic is also covered in Chapter 6];

and (3) damages suffered in connection with effecting cover.

EXAMPLE 1. S in Chicago and B in Peoria enter into a contract for the sale by S of a 1966 baby grand Soundway piano for $5000. S is to pay for the cost of shipping the piano from Chicago to Peoria. S repudiates the contract. B, who wishes to cover, places an ad in a trade journal, (at a cost of $100) and locates a substitute Soundway in Detroit for $6000. Under the terms of his contract with the Detroit seller, B is to pay for the cost of shipping the piano from Detroit to Peoria, $300. B sues. Under UCC 2–712, B may recover the contract price-cover cost differential ($1000) plus the incidental damages suffered in connection with effecting cover ($100 in advertising costs plus $300 in shipment costs).

EXAMPLE 2. Same facts but S ships a piano to B which does not conform to the contract. When B receives the piano, he immediately becomes aware of the nonconformity. He therefore rightfully rejects it and ships it back to S at his (B's) own expense, $250. On the day B learns of the breach, the market price for 1966 baby grand Soundway pianos is $5800. B chooses not to cover; but, instead brings suit pursuant to UCC 2–713. In addition to the contract-market differential ($800), B may recover as incidental damages the cost associated with rightful rejection of the piano ($250).

§ 5.5 Consequential Damages, UCC 2–715

Consequential damages are, likewise, recoverable by buyer under UCC 2–712 and 2–713. According to UCC 2–715(2)(a), "Consequential damages resulting from the seller's breach include any loss resulting from general or particular requirements and needs of which the seller at the time of contracting had reason to know and which could not reasonably be prevented by cover or otherwise."

(a) Types of Consequential Damages

The most frequently sought-after types of consequential damages are (1) lost profits and (2) damages resulting from liability to third persons.

Lost Profits

The vast majority of cases involving consequential damages arise in the context of an aggrieved buyer who is attempting to recover profits from other transactions which were allegedly prevented by virtue of seller's breach. (See e. g. Illustration in § 1.1(d) supra).

Damages Resulting from Liability to Third Persons

A seller's breach of contract may cause a buyer to become liable to third persons by virtue of the fact that the goods involved were supposed to be resold to and/or used by persons other than buyer. In such cases, subject to the rules set forth in subsections (b) through (e) infra, buyer may recover as consequential damages payments made to third persons to whom buyer was under legal obligation.

EXAMPLE 1. Seller and buyer enter into a contract for the sale of webbing to be used in the manufacture of army leggings. At the time of contracting, seller knows that buyer is already under contract to manufacture and deliver the leggings to the army. Seller repudiates the agreement. Because buyer is unable to cover, he is forced to breach his contract with the army, which results in a lawsuit by the army against buyer. Buyer may recover from seller as consequential damages the amount of his liability resulting from breach of the army contract.

EXAMPLE 2. Shipowner contracts with farmer for the sale of a large supply of lemons, limes, and oranges. At the time of contracting, farmer knows that shipowner intends to feed the fruit to his crew in order to prevent scurvy, a disease which is caused by a vitamin C deficiency. Farmer repudiates the agreement, and shipowner is unable to effect cover. As a result, several members of his crew become afflicted with scurvy, and they bring suit against shipowner. Shipowner may re-

[*152*]

cover from farmer as consequential damages the amount of payments he is obligated to make to his afflicted crew members.

(b) Foreseeability

UCC 2–715 tracks the "rule at common law which . . . [makes] the seller liable for all consequential damages of which he had 'reason to know' in advance." UCC 2–715, Official Comment #2. "Particular needs of the buyer must generally be made known to the seller while general needs must rarely be known to charge the seller with knowledge." UCC 2–715, Official Comment #3. Moreover, "in the case of sale of wares to one in the business of reselling them, resale is one of the [general] requirements of which the seller has reason to know." UCC 2–715 Official Comment #6. [See generally § 1.3 supra for a discussion of the foreseeability requirement].

(c) Causation

Consequential damages are recoverable only if they are proximately caused by defendant's breach. [See generally § 1.4, supra for a discussion of the causation requirement].

(d) Reasonable Certainty

Consequential damages are not recoverable when they are uncertain or speculative. In the general discussion of the "certainty" requirement, [see §

1.5 supra], it was noted that some courts apply that term liberally, while others require something approaching mathematical precision in establishing proof of damages. Official Comment #4 to section UCC 2-715 makes it clear that the Code has opted for the liberal approach: "The burden of proving the extent of loss incurred by way of consequential damage is on the buyer, but the section on liberal administration of remedies [UCC 1-106] rejects any doctrine of certainty which requires almost mathematical precision in the proof of loss. Loss may be determined in any manner which is reasonable under the circumstances."

New Versus Established Businesses

As is the case in non-sales contracts [see § 1.5(c) supra], if defendant's breach has prevented plaintiff from operating all or part of an already established business, lost profits on transactions prevented by the breach will generally be provable with reasonable certainty. On the other hand, if seller's breach has prevented buyer from opening a new business, consequential damages (lost profits) will generally be held to be too speculative to be recoverable. [c.f. EXAMPLES set forth in § 1.5(c)].

Goods Which Buyer Has Purchased for Resale

When an aggrieved buyer has contracted to purchase goods for the purpose of reselling them, and this fact is known to seller, the amount of resale profits prevented by the breach will generally be provable with reasonable certainty.

EXAMPLE. Manufacturer and retailer enter into a contract for the sale of three Soundway grand pianos for $6000 each. At the time of contracting, manufacturer knows that retailer intends to resell the pianos, and that there is a resale market for Soundways in buyer's area. If manufacturer breaches the contract, and retailer is unable to cover [see subsection (e) infra], lost profits based on the resale market price in buyer's area will be recoverable.

Loss of Good will

In most jurisdictions, the courts will not grant recovery under the UCC for consequential damages resulting from a loss of customer good will. In denying recovery for this type of loss, one court stated that "there is no indication that the Uniform Commercial Code was intended to enlarge the scope of a buyer's damages to include a loss of good will. In the absence of a specific declaration in this respect, we believe that damages of this nature would be entirely too speculative . . ."

(e) Inability to Mitigate by Cover or Otherwise

The Code imposes the principle of mitigation of damages upon the recovery of consequential damages. UCC 2–715(2)(a) specifically states that there can be recovery only for consequential losses "which could not *reasonably* be prevented by cover or otherwise." [emphasis added]. This section apparently incorporates the common law rule that buyer has the duty to mitigate ["by cover or otherwise"] only if he can do so "by reasonable effort, without undue risk, expense, or humiliation." [See § 1.2(b) supra].

EXAMPLE 1. Shipowner contracts with farmer for the sale of a large supply of lemons, limes, and oranges which he intends to feed to his crew in order to prevent scurvy. At the time of farmer's repudiation, there are substitute lemons, limes, and oranges available on the market which shipowner could purchase with reasonable effort and without undue expense. However, shipowner fails to cover and several crew members who become afflicted with scurvy bring suit against shipowner. Shipowner may not recover from farmer as consequential damages the amount of payments he is obligated to make to his afflicted crew members.

EXAMPLE 2. Same facts but shipowner pays farmer in advance. When farmer repudiates, he fails to return the purchase price for a three month period. Although there is substitute fruit available on the market, shipowner does not have sufficient capital available to "cover" unless he borrows at an extremely high interest rate. Since this would involve "unreasonable expense," shipowner has no duty to cover and may recover the consequential damages from farmer.

§ 5.6 Specific Performance, Replevin, and Recovery of Goods from Insolvent Seller

Money damages will not always be an adequate remedy for an aggrieved buyer. In certain circumstances only an equitable remedy will suffice. In such cases the aggrieved buyer may be entitled to (1) specific performance, or (2) replevin, or (3) in the event of seller's insolvency, recovery of the goods.

(a) Specific Performance, UCC 2-716(1) and (2)

UCC 2-716 provides that "specific performance may be decreed where the goods are unique or in other proper circumstances." According to Official Comment #2, "the test of uniqueness under this section must be made in terms of the total situation which characterizes the contract. . . . However, uniqueness is not the sole basis of the remedy under this section for the relief may also be granted 'in other proper circumstances'; and inability to cover is strong evidence of 'other proper circumstances.' "

EXAMPLE 1. Retailer and manufacturer enter into a contract whereby manufacturer will supply retailer with the latter's requirements for hoola hoops. Manufacturer repudiates the agreement. Retailer sues and requests a decree of specific performance on the grounds that there is no other supplier from which she can obtain a large quantity of hoola hoops. The decree will be granted.

According to Official Comment #2, "output and requirements contracts involving a particular or peculiarly available source or market present today the typical commercial specific performance situation," either because the absence of another source of supply indicates that the goods are "unique" or because the "inability to cover is strong evidence of 'other proper circumstances.'"

EXAMPLE 2. Manufacturer, as part of a close-out sale, contracts to supply retailer with hoola hoops at an extremely low price. When manufacturer repudiates the agreement, there are substitute hoola hoops available but at a much higher price. Retailer sues and requests a decree of specific performance. The decree will not be granted. It is only the "close-out" price of the goods which is unique; not the goods themselves. Cover is possible; therefore specific performance is an inappropriate remedy.

Election of Remedies Not Required

The remedy of specific performances does not preclude damages or other relief. UCC 2–716(2) provides that "the decree for specific performance may include such terms and conditions as to payment of the price, damages, or other relief as the court may deem just."

(b) Replevin, UCC 2–716(3)

UCC 2–716(3) gives the buyer rights to the goods comparable to the seller's right to the price [see

Chapter 7]. The buyer has a "right of replevin for goods identified to the contract if after reasonable effort he is unable to effect cover for such goods or the circumstances reasonably indicate that such an effort will be unavailing." This subsection appears to add nothing to subsection (1), under which the "inability to cover is strong evidence of 'other proper circumstances'" under which a court will decree specific performance. UCC 2–716, Official Comment #2.

(c) Recovery of Goods from Insolvent Seller, UCC 2–502

When a seller is insolvent, damages usually are not an adequate remedy for the buyer because he will be unable to collect them. While such a buyer may use the remedies listed in §§ 5.2 and 5.3, the Code provides an additional remedy that is more beneficial to the buyer. Under UCC 2–502, if the buyer has paid part of the price and the seller has become insolvent within ten days after receipt of the first installment of the payment, the buyer may recover the goods that have been identified to the contract by tendering the balance due.

Purpose of Ten Day Limitation Period

The ten-day limitation recognizes that other creditors of the insolvent seller also need protection. In balancing the rights of the buyer against those of the seller's other creditors, the Code gives a preference to the buyer for a short period of time, because an imminently insolvent seller who accepts part of the price will probably be unable to perform his side of the bargain and thus is acting in a manner that is close to being fraudulent. The longer the time between the receipt by the seller of part of the price and the moment he becomes insolvent, however, the lesser the likelihood that there has been a fraud. In the absence of fraud, there is no reason for giving buyer a preference over seller's other creditors.

CHAPTER 6

REMEDIES AVAILABLE TO BUYER AFTER HE HAS ACCEPTED THE GOODS, INCLUDING REMEDIES FOR BREACH OF WARRANTY

When a seller delivers goods which "fail in any respect to conform to the contract, the buyer may (a) reject the whole; or (b) accept the whole; or (c) accept any commercial unit or units and reject the rest." UCC 2-601. If the buyer chooses to reject the non-conforming goods, the remedies discussed in Chapter 5 are applicable. If the goods are accepted, the remedies discussed in §§ 6.3 and 6.4 infra apply.

§ 6.1 Definition of Acceptance and Rejection

The terms "acceptance" and "rejection" are given statutory definitions in UCC 2-606 and UCC 2-602 respectively.

(a) Acceptance, UCC 2-606

The term is defined by UCC 2-606(1) which provides that: "Acceptance of goods occurs when the buyer (a) after a reasonable opportunity to inspect the goods signifies to the seller that the goods are conforming or that he will take or retain them in spite of their nonconformity; or (b) fails to make an effective rejection . . . but such acceptance does not occur until the buyer has had a reasonable opportunity to inspect them; or (c) does any act inconsistent with the seller's ownership."

(b) Rejection, UCC 2-602

A rejection occurs when the buyer signifies to the seller that he will not take or retain the goods. Rejection requires affirmative action on the part of the buyer. If he does nothing after having had a reasonable opportunity to inspect the goods, he will be deemed to have accepted them. "Rejection of goods must be within a reasonable time after their delivery or tender. It is ineffective unless buyer seasonably notifies the seller." UCC 2-602(1).

§ 6.2   Revocation of Acceptance, UCC 2-608

As will be discussed below, the buyer who accepts nonconforming goods is given remedies which are different from, and usually inferior to, those available to the rejecting buyer. Because the accepting buyer's remedies are usually not as satisfactory, the Code allows him, in limited circumstances, to revoke his acceptance and place himself in the position he would have occupied had he initially rejected the goods.

(a) Effect of Revocation

The effect of revocation of acceptance is to place the buyer in the same position he would have occupied if he had rejected the goods at the outset. Thus, a buyer properly revoking acceptance can "cover" under UCC 2–712, recover damages for non-delivery under UCC 2–713, and obtain specific performance in a proper case under UCC 2–716. Such a remedial position is generally more satisfactory than that of the accepting buyer, because the latter is stuck with the goods and the obligation to pay for them at the contract rate. [See § 6.3 infra].

(b) Grounds for Revocation

Revocation of acceptance is governed by UCC 2–608 which provides that the buyer may revoke his acceptance of *goods whose non-conformity substantially impairs their value to him* if: (a) he accepted the goods on the reasonable assumption that the non-conformity would be cured and it has not been seasonably cured; or (b) he accepted the goods without discovering their defects due to the difficulty of discovery or to the seller's assurances.

Substantial Impairment of Value: Elimination of Foreseeability Requirement

"Revocation of acceptance is possible only where the non-conformity substantially impairs the value of the goods to the buyer. For this purpose the test is *not* what the seller had reason to know at the time of contracting; the question is whether the non-conformity is such as will *in fact* cause a substantial impairment of value to the buyer though the seller had no advance knowledge as to the buyer's particular circumstances." UCC 2–608, Official Comment #2. [Emphasis supplied]. The drafters of the Code did not disclose their rationale for omitting the foreseeability requirement when measuring the substantiality of impairment of value.

Seller's Failure to Cure

The first circumstance justifying buyer's revocation of acceptance is when he has been misled into accepting defective goods on the reasonable assumption (usually caused by seller's assurances) that the nonconformities would be cured and the seller then fails to cure. The rationale for this rule is that the buyer would have rejected the goods at the outset but for the seller's assurances of cure. Thus, the buyer must be permitted to revoke his acceptance in order to occupy the same remedial position he would have been in had he rejected initially.

Latent Defects

The second circumstance justifying revocation of acceptance is the buyer's failure to discover the non-conformity because of its latent nature. When revocation is made on these grounds, the buyer's expertise, sophistication and occupation will all be relevant in making a determination of whether there was "difficulty of discovery [of the defect] before acceptance."

EXAMPLE. S, an airplane salesman, and B, a consumer, enter into a contract for the sale of an airplane. During negotiations, S and his mechanic represent the plane to be airworthy and free from defects. B has a pilot's license but is not a mechanic and has no mechanical training other than that required as a condition of obtaining a license. Before purchasing the airplane, B test-flies it and has no difficulty with it. Two weeks after accepting delivery of the plane, B begins experiencing difficulty with the engine. The difficulty is caused by a defect which, although not revealed during B's test flight, could have been discovered by a skilled mechanic. B may revoke his acceptance of the airplane. Given B's lack of mechanical expertise, B's acceptance was reasonably induced both by "the difficulty of discovery before acceptance" *and* "by the seller's assurances."

Seller's Assurances Against Defects

Finally, the buyer may revoke his acceptance on the grounds that the seller has assured him that there were no defects. The rationale behind this rule is that seller's assurances may have prevented immediate discovery of the defects by inducing buyer to accept quickly and without making an adequate inspection. Here, as in the immediately preceding section, the buyer's skill, expertise, and occupation are relevant in making a determination of whether buyer's acceptance was "reasonably in-

duced . . . by the seller's assurances." One
question left open by the Code is whether one can
revoke an acceptance induced by assurances contained in seller's advertisements. It is at least
arguable that such a buyer is not acting reasonably if he fails to make further inquiry or inspection and that, therefore, revocation should not be
permitted.

(c) Conditions for Revocation

UCC 2–608(2) sets forth three conditions which
must be met before an effective revocation can be
made. These are: (a) Revocation of acceptance
must occur *within a reasonable time* after the
buyer discovers or should have discovered the
ground for it; (b) It must occur before any substantial change in condition of the goods which is
not caused by their own defects; (c) It is not
effective until the buyer notifies the seller of it.

Must Occur Within a Reasonable Time

The "reasonable time" for revocation of acceptance does not run until "the buyer discovers or
should have discovered the defect." What length
of time is reasonable will depend not only on the
difficulty of discovery but also on the course of
dealings between the parties after acceptance but
before formal revocation of acceptance.

EXAMPLE. S and B contract for the sale of an
irrigation machine. B accepts delivery of the ma-

chine. Immediately after installation on March 1,
B becomes aware of numerous mechanical defects,
and immediately notifies S that the machine will
not operate. During the following three months, S
makes several attempts to repair the machine, but
all these efforts are unsuccessful. Consequently B
is unable to use the machine to irrigate her crop.
On June 15, B notifies S of her revocation of acceptance. On substantially similar facts, several
courts have held that the revocation was timely.
Noting that one of the policies behind the "reasonable time" requirement is to give seller an opportunity to cure the defect, the courts have stated
that this policy is fostered by the buyer's complaint and the seller's attempted repairs prior to
formal revocation of acceptance. The following
language of one such court is typical: "Here, the
buyer gave the seller an opportunity to repair the
machine and withheld his revocation of acceptance
until it became apparent that seller could not or
would not perform its contract. Under the circumstances of this case, the delay in the notice in no
way prejudiced the seller and the delay was not
unreasonable."

Before Any Substantial Change in Condition Which is Not Caused by a Defect in the Goods

The gist of this requirement is that the revocation must be made before the goods have substan-

tially depreciated in value either because of their perishability or because of the decrease in market value which is normally incident to the age and use of goods.

EXAMPLE. S, an airplane salesman, and B, a consumer, enter into a contract for the sale of an airplane. During negotiations, S and his mechanic represent the plane to be airworthy and free from defects. B flies the airplane for one year and 500,000 miles before discovering the latent defect in the engine. B may not revoke his acceptance; there has been a substantial change in the condition of the airplane (i. e. in its age and in the fact that it has been flown 500,000 miles) not caused by its defects. B's revocation of acceptance is ineffective. B will not have the remedies which the Code gives to those who reject goods. Instead, he will have only those remedies, discussed below, available to buyers who have accepted nonconforming goods.

Revocation Not Effective Until Buyer Notifies Seller of It

There is a split of authority as to whether the mere return of nonconforming goods to the seller constitutes sufficient notification of revocation. Many courts have held that it does not; and that the buyer must, in addition, unequivocally notify the seller in writing that he is revoking his acceptance due to the defect in the goods or their other

nonconformity to the contract. In those jurisdictions, the notification must occur within a reasonable time.

(d) Rights of Buyer Who Revokes Acceptance

A buyer who effectively revokes his acceptance
has the same rights with respect to the goods involved as if he had rejected them at the outset.
UCC 2-608(3). Thus, the entire range of remedies
set forth in Chapter Five is available to the revoking buyer. The accepting buyer, on the other
hand, is given only those remedies discussed in the
immediately following sections.

§ 6.3 The Accepting Buyer's Rights to Recoup-
ment and Damages

After the buyer accepts the goods, he must pay
for them at the contract rate. UCC 2-607(1).
However, the accepting buyer is not entirely
without recourse against the breaching seller. Although he is "stuck" with goods which may be of
little or no value to him, he is entitled to recoup
damages under UCC 2-717. In addition, if buyer's
damages exceed the balance of the price which he
owes to seller, buyer may affirmatively recover
damages pursuant to UCC 2-714.

(a) Recoupment, UCC 2-717

"The buyer on notifying the seller of his intention to do so may deduct all or any part of the

damages resulting from any part of the price still due under the same contract." UCC 2–717. The buyer's right to recoupment is not limited to breach of warranty cases but is available whenever seller fails in any way to perform his obligations under the contract.

(b) Recovery of Damages, UCC 2–714

Recoupment is a satisfactory remedy only in those cases where the amount of damages sustained by buyer is less than or equal to amount of the price still due under the contract. In the event that buyer's damages exceed the unpaid balance of the price, he may, in addition to recoupment, "recover as damages for any nonconformity of tender the loss resulting in the ordinary course of events from the seller's breach as determined in any manner which is reasonable." UCC 2–714(1). "The nonconformity referred to in [this section] includes not only breaches of warranties but also any failure of the seller to perform his obligations under the contract." UCC 2–714, Official Comment #2.

Notice

Where the goods have been accepted, "the buyer must within a reasonable time after he discovers or should have discovered any breach notify the seller of breach or be barred from any remedy." UCC 2–607(3)(a).

The notification necessary, to preserve the buyer's rights to any remedies for breach need merely be sufficient to let the seller know that the transaction is troublesome, and that a way for the parties is open for normal settlement through negotiation. Neither a clear statement of all the buyer's objections nor a threat of litigation is required for a proper notice. UCC 2–607, Official Comment #4.

A notice that would not be sufficient for purposes of revoking an acceptance may be sufficient for purposes of allowing the buyer to pursue his post-acceptance remedies. Both UCC 2–608(2) (revocation of acceptance) and UCC 2–607(3)(a) (notice as a prerequisite to post-acceptance remedies) use the words "reasonable time" to describe the period in which buyer must notify seller. However, the purposes of the sections are different and it is clear that a notice which may be too late to satisfy UCC 2–608 may be timely for purposes of 2–607. For example, in the example involving the airplane which has been flown 500,000 miles before discovery of the defect, an attempted revocation of acceptance by B would not be timely because there has been a substantial change in the condition of the airplane due to use and depreciation. However, if B gives notice within a reasonable time after discovering the defect in the engine, the notice will be sufficient to preserve B's post-acceptance remedies against S.

Measure of Damages

When a buyer has accepted a nonconforming tender and seeks damages under UCC 2-714, the seller must be given credit for the value to the buyer of the accepted goods. Normally the measure of damages is the difference between the value of the goods and the value they would have had if they had conformed to the contract. In addition, "in a proper case any incidental and consequential damages . . . may also be recovered." UCC 2-714(3). [See §§ 5.4 and 5.5 supra for a discussion of incidental and consequential damages]. While the accepting buyer is, theoretically, given adequate protection through his rights of recoupment and damages, as an actual matter he is often not in as good a position as he would have occupied had he either rejected the goods initially or effectively revoked his acceptance. This inadequacy of protection arises from the fact that the credit given to seller for goods accepted by the buyer is measured objectively and may exceed the value which they actually have to buyer. [See Example in § 6.4(b) infra].

§ 6.4 Buyer's Damages for Breach of Warranty, UCC 2-714

UCC 2-714(2) sets forth a formula for measuring damages for breach of warranty with respect to goods which have been accepted. The following subsections will discuss that statutory formula and the problems which often arise in its application.

(a) Statutory Formula: Difference Between Value as Warranted and Value as Accepted

"The measure of damages for breach of warranty is the difference at the time and place of acceptance between the value of the goods accepted and the value they would have had if they had been as warranted, unless special circumstances show proximate damages of a different amount." UCC 2–714(2). The two most frequent methods of measuring the difference between the value as warranted and the value as accepted are: (1) cost of repair and (2) contract price minus resale price.

Cost of Repair

If the defective portion of the goods can be repaired or replaced, then the differential can be computed simply by ascertaining the cost of repair and/or replacement of the defective parts.

EXAMPLE. S and B enter into a contract for the sale of a new car for $6,000. The contract contains all the standard warranties, express and implied. B accepts the car and pays the entire purchase price. Upon discovering that the radiator is cracked and the brakes are defective, B decides not to revoke his acceptance [See § 6.2 supra]. Instead, he has the radiator replaced (at a cost of $500) and the brakes repaired (at a cost of $100).

After taking these actions, the car is in as good a condition as it would have been had it been delivered "as warranted." Hence the "difference . . . between the value of the goods accepted and the value they would have had if they had been as warranted" is $600.

Contract Price Minus Resale Price

In many breach of warranty cases the defect is irreparable. In such cases it is, of course, not possible to measure buyer's damages by cost of repair. In such cases some courts have held that the value of the goods as warranted can be measured by the contract price itself; and the value of the goods accepted can be measured by the amount buyer can (or could) obtain by prompt resale.

EXAMPLE 1. Farmer and Grocer enter into a contract for the sale of Grade A tomatoes, warranted to be in perfect condition, for $2000. However, when the tomatoes are delivered Grocer discovers that they are badly bruised. Instead of rejecting them, Grocer accepts delivery and promptly resells the tomatoes to a ketchup company for a reasonable price, $800. In such a case many courts would hold that the strongest evidence of the value of the goods as warranted is the contract price itself ($2000); moreover, the most appropriate measure of the value of the goods accepted is their resale price ($800). Therefore, Grocer's damages under UCC 2–714(2) amount to $1,200.

EXAMPLE 2. Farmer and Butcher enter into a contract for the sale of beef cows, for $10,000. After accepting delivery of the cows, Butcher discovers that they are contaminated with PBB. The cows are immediately quarantined and eventually die. Butcher sues for breach of warranty under UCC 2–714(2). The measure of damages is the difference between the value of the goods as warranted (measured by the contract price of $10,000) and the value of the goods accepted (0).

(b) "Value of Goods Accepted": Objective Standards

As previously noted, the accepting buyer is sometimes not placed in as good a position as he would have occupied had he either rejected the goods initially or effectively revoked his acceptance. This inadequacy of protection arises from the fact that the credit given to seller for goods accepted by buyer is measured objectively and may exceed the value which they actually have to buyer.

EXAMPLE. Vladimir, a world-famous pianist, contracts to have a Soundway piano delivered to him in East Podunk where he is scheduled to give a concert. The Soundway is warranted to have a "tight action" which is the type preferred by Vladimir.

When the piano is delivered, Vladimir immediately discovers that the piano has a very "loose action." He cannot, however, reject the piano because he needs it for his concert which is scheduled for the next day. While the looseness of the action does, in fact, impair Vladimir's performance, there is no difference in objective value between a piano with a "tight" action and one with a "loose" one; it is simply a matter of individual preference. A suit under UCC 2-714(2) will probably yield no recovery for Vladimir. Theoretically, the provisions of UCC 2-714 are stated with sufficient broadness to permit a finding that the value to Vladimir of the goods accepted was much less than the value as warranted. However, the courts have almost universally taken the position that the seller is to be given credit measured by the objective value that the accepted ("defective") goods have generally. Moreover, while consequential damages (loss of Vladimir's popularity with his "fans") are perhaps foreseeable (see §§ 1.3 and 5.5(b) supra), they are highly speculative (see § 1.5 and § 5.5(d) supra) and hence probably not recoverable. (Note: At least one commentator has argued that the value of goods accepted "is a personalized criterion designed to allow the buyer to offer special evidence of the needs of his own enterprise and resources and to show that the goods accepted are less valuable to him than their market value price would otherwise indicate." However, this view has not been generally accepted by the courts).

(c) "Special Circumstances Show[ing] Proximate Damages of a Different Amount"

As discussed in the immediately preceding section, the courts have not been willing to use subjective criteria in measuring "value of goods accepted." If the courts chose to do so, they could still arrive at a personalized outcome through a broad interpretation of the final clause of UCC 2–714(2) which authorizes a different measure of damages if "special circumstances show proximate damages of a different amount." However, none of the cases interpreting the "special circumstances" clause of UCC 2–714(2) have used that clause to arrive at a subjective measure of "value of goods accepted." Instead, those few courts which have interpreted the term "special circumstances" have simply stated that it is a pre-requisite for the recovery of incidental and consequential damages under UCC 2–714(3). This narrow interpretation of "special circumstances" seems inconsistent with the wording and organizational structure of UCC 2–714.

(d) Incidental and Consequential Damages

UCC 2–714(3) authorizes the recovery of incidental and consequential damages in "proper case(s)." These damages are recoverable not only in breach of warranty cases but also in any other case where buyer is seeking damages with respect to goods which he has accepted. [See § 1.1(d) for a general discussion of consequential damages and §§ 5.4 and 5.5 for rules governing recovery of incidental and consequential damages in contracts for the sale of goods].

(e) *Modification or Limitation of Remedies for Breach of Warranty*

UCC 2-316(4) provides that "remedies for breach of warranty can be limited in accordance with the provisions of this article on liquidation or limitation of damages and on contractual modification of remedy [UCC 2-718 and 2-719]". [See generally Chapter 9 for a discussion of liquidated damages under UCC 2-718, and Chapter 10 for the rules pertaining to contractual modification or limitation of remedy under UCC 2-719].

CHAPTER 7

REMEDIES AVAILABLE TO SELLER WHEN BUYER DEFAULTS AND HAS NOT ACCEPTED THE GOODS

UCC 2-703 gathers together all of the various remedies available to a seller for any breach by a buyer who has not accepted the goods or has wrongfully revoked his acceptance. According to that statutory section, the aggrieved seller may (a) withhold delivery; (b) stop delivery by any bailee (UCC 2-705); (c) identify goods to the contract or salvage unfinished goods (UCC 2-704); (d) re-sell and recover damages (UCC 2-706); (e) recover damages for non-acceptance (UCC 2-708) or in a proper case for the price (UCC 2-709); (f) cancel.

§ 7.1 Election of Remedies Not Required

Article 2 of the UCC "rejects any doctrine of election of remedy as a fundamental policy and thus the remedies [listed in UCC 2-703] are essentially cumulative in nature and include all of the available remedies for breach. Whether the pursuit of one remedy bars another depends entirely on the facts of the individual case." UCC 2-703, Official Comment #1.

While it is thus clear that some of the seller's *remedies* are cumulative (for example—cancelling, withholding delivery, and suing for damages, could all co-exist in one action), the four statutory formulae for measuring seller's *expectation damages* appear to be mutually exclusive. That is, an aggrieved seller's pre-acceptance damages will be measured *either* by 2–706, *or* by 2–708(1), *or* by 2–708(2), *or* by 2–709. These four alternative formulae for measuring expectation damages are explored in §§ 7.2 through 7.5. The final three sections in this Chapter (§§ 7.6 through 7.8) will be devoted to the seller's right to recover incidental damages, his right to salvage unfinished goods, and his rights against the insolvent buyer.

§ 7.2   Seller's Resale, UCC 2–706

This section authorizes an aggrieved seller to resell the goods and to recover damages measured by the difference between the contract price and the resale price, together with incidental damages but less any expenses saved in consequence of buyer's breach.

EXAMPLE. Seller, in Chicago, contracts to sell furniture to a New York buyer for $50,000. Under the terms of the contract, seller is to pay the shipping cost of $1000. Buyer repudiates; and seller, after placing an ad in a trade journal (at a cost of $300) is able to resell in Chicago for $46,000. Under this resale contract, seller will pay no shipping or delivery costs. Seller's net proceeds under the original contract would have been $49,000. Under the resale contract, his net proceeds will be $45,700. Therefore, given the goal of placing seller in as good a position as he would have been in had the contract not been breached, seller's recovery should be $3,300. The formula set forth in UCC 2–706, leads to the same result: Contract price ($50,000) minus resale price ($46,000) plus incidental damages ($300 for advertisement) less expenses saved ($1000 shipping costs). $50,000 − $46,000 + $300 − $1,000 = $3,300.

(a) Analogous to Buyer's Right to Cover

Section 2–706 is the seller's remedial equivalent to the buyer's right to "cover" (UCC 2–712, § 5.2 supra); and, as is the case with "cover", resale is not mandatory. When the seller does choose to resell, he may do so at either a private or public sale. A public sale is a "sale by auction." UCC 2–706, Official Comment #4.

(b) Conditions for Commercially Reasonable Private and Public Resales

If the seller chooses to resell *privately*, he must (a) identify the resale contract to the broken contract; (b) resell in good faith and in a commercially reasonable manner; and (c) give the buyer reasonable notification of his intention to resell. UCC 2–706(2), (3).

If the seller chooses to resell *publicly*, he must (a) identify the resale contract to the broken contract; (b) resell in good faith and in a commercially reasonably manner; (c) resell only identified goods unless there is a recognized market for a public sale of futures in goods of the kind; (d) conduct the resale at the usual place for a public sale, if there is such a place; (e) give the buyer reasonable notice of the time and place of resale except in the case of perishable goods which threaten to decline in value rapidly; and (f) keep the goods on view at the time of sale, or notify those attending the sale where the goods are located and provide for reasonable inspection by prospective bidders. UCC 2-706(4).

(c) Good Faith Purchaser's Rights

UCC 2-706(5) provides that a good faith purchaser at a resale takes the goods free of any rights of the original buyer even though the seller fails to comply with one or more of the requirements of UCC 2-706.

(d) Failure to Make Commercially Reasonable Resale

If the seller does not follow the steps set forth in subsection (b) supra, he will be deprived of the right to use the UCC 2-706 formula as his measure of damages.   His non-compliance will, in effect, relegate him to the position of one who has not resold, and his damages will be measured in accordance with the formula set forth in UCC 2-708 (1) which is discussed in the immediately following section. (But see Example in § 7.3(a) infra for an exception to this rule).

§ 7.3   Difference Between Contract Price and Market Price, UCC 2-708(1)

After a default by buyer, the seller may choose not to resell. In such a case, he is entitled to recover damages based on the difference between the unpaid contract price and the prevailing market price at the time and place for tender, together with incidental damages, but less any expense saved as a result of buyer's breach. This section gives seller a remedy equivalent to the buyer's right to compute damages by using the contract price-market price differential. [UCC 2-713, § 5.3 supra].

(a) Alternative Remedy to UCC 2-706

The remedy provided by UCC 2-706 (Resale) and the one provided by 2-708(1) (Contract-market differential) are mutually exclusive. If the aggrieved seller chooses to resell the goods, his statutory remedy is 2-706. If he chooses not to resell, his statutory remedy is 2-708(1). Moreover, although there appears to be no case law in point, the better reasoned view seems to be that the seller who has chosen to resell cannot bypass the steps set forth in 2-706 (See § 7.2(b)) and sue for the contract-market differential in the event that the latter would yield a larger recovery.

EXAMPLE. Seller and buyer enter into a contract for the sale of furniture for $50,000. Buyer repudiates. The market price at the time and place for tender is $42,000; thus the contract-market differential under 2–708(1) would be $8,000. However, two weeks after the time set for tender, seller resells the furniture at a private sale for $48,000 and purposely fails to give buyer notice of his intended resale. Had seller notified buyer, his recovery under UCC 2–706 would, of course, be only $2,000. If he purposely (or even unintentionally) fails to comply with the requirements of 2–706, he should not be permitted to sue under UCC 2–708(1) and recover $8,000 in damages. To permit such a recovery, of course, be to place the "aggrieved" seller in a better position than he would have been in had the buyer not breached the contract.

(b) Exception to Mitigation Doctrine

As is the case with the buyer's remedy provided by UCC 2–713 (§ 5.3 supra), UCC 2–708(1) is a statutory exception to the principle that an aggrieved party must mitigate his damages (See § 1.2 supra). That is, an aggrieved seller is under no duty to resell, even if by reselling he could have avoided the consequences of the statutory damages imposed by UCC 2–708(1).

EXAMPLE. On April 1, during a period when the market price for coffee is rapidly fluctuating, S and B enter into a contract for the sale of 3000 pounds of coffee at $2.50 per pound. On the date set for tender, when the market price has fallen to

$2.00 per pound, B repudiates the contract. One week later the market price climbs to $2.40. Nevertheless, S chooses not to resell, and instead sues for damages under 2–708(1). S may recover $1500, the difference between the contract price ($7500) and the market price ($6000) at the time and place for tender. This is true even though S could have avoided most of this loss by reselling the coffee one week after the breach at $2.40 per pound. If S had mitigated damages by reselling at that price, his damages, governed by UCC 2–706, would have been the difference between the contract price ($7500) and the resale price ($7200) or $300. Because the statutory scheme provided by UCC 2–706 and UCC 2–708(1) does not impose on S the duty to mitigate by reselling, S can recover the entire market-contract differential, $1500.

(c) Time and Place for Determining Market Price

The aggrieved seller's "contract-market" damages are measured by the market price prevailing at the *time and place for tender*. It should be noted that in this respect the aggrieved seller is treated differently from the aggrieved buyer. The *buyer's* "contract-market" damages [UCC 2–713, see § 5.3 (d) supra] are measured by the market price at the *time when buyer learns of the breach*, using as a yardstick the market in which the buyer could have obtained cover had he sought to do so. While the Official Comments to UCC 2–708(1) do not explain this disparity in treatment, there seems to be a good reason for it. Assuming that it was the intention of the drafters of UCC 2-708 (1) to use as a yardstick the market in which the seller could have resold had he chosen to do so, the market price prevailing at the time seller learned of the breach would be an inappropriate baseline. For, if the seller is a manufacturer, he may not have completed the goods by the date on which he learns of the breach; and if he is a wholesaler or retailer, he may not have obtained the goods by that date. The earliest date on which all sellers will (or should) have obtained or completed manufacture of the goods (and, therefore, could have resold them if they had chosen to do so) will be the date set for tender. This is apparently the reason why the code fixes the "time for tender" as the time for determining the aggrieved seller's market damages.

Evidence of Market Price at Other Times and Places

"If evidence of a price prevailing at the times or places described [UCC 2-708(1)] is not readily available, the price prevailing within any reasonable time before or after the time described or in any other place which in commercial judgment or under usage of the trade would serve as a reasonable substitute . . . may be used, making any proper allowance for the cost of transporting goods to or from such place." UCC 2-723(2).

Admissibility of Market Quotations

Market quotations published in official publications, trade journals, newspapers or periodicals of general circulation are admissible in evidence where the prevailing price of goods bought or sold in any established commodity market is in issue. UCC 2-724.

§ 7.4   Lost Profits, UCC 2-708(2)

UCC 2-708(2) provides: "If the measure of damages provided in subsection (1) is inadequate to put the seller in as good a position as performance would have done then the measure of damages is the profit (including reasonable overhead) which the seller would have made from full performance by the buyer . . ."

(a) The Lost Volume Seller

The primary purpose of UCC 2-708(2) is to provide compensation for a certain type of seller—the volume seller. "The normal measure . . . would be the list price less cost to the dealer or list price less manufacturing cost to the manufacturer." [UCC 2-708, Official Comment #2].

EXAMPLE. S, a car dealer, contracts with B for the sale of a Pink Panther automobile. The list price (and contract price) is $5000. B breaches and S resells that automobile to X for $5000 which is the prevailing market price. However, X intended to buy a Pink Panther from S even if B had not breached; and S's supply of Pink Panthers exceeds the current demand. If the cost to the dealer of each Pink Panther is $4000, then (had B not breached the contract), S would have made a $1000 profit on the sale to B and an additional $1000 profit on the sale to X. Clearly the "contract-market" remedy provided by UCC 2–708(1) is inadequate to compensate S because it would give him no damages at all. The formula provided by UCC 2–706 (See § 7.2 supra) would, likewise, yield no recovery. The only way to put S "in as good a position as performance would have done" is to award him his lost profit, or $1000.

§ 7.5　Action for the Price, UCC 2–709

UCC 2–709(1)(b) provides that where the buyer fails to pay the price as it becomes due, "the seller may recover, together with any incidental damages .　.　.　the price of goods identified to the contract [See UCC 2–501(1)] if *[after reasonable effort] the seller is unable to resell them at a reasonable price* or the circumstances reasonably indicate that such effort will be unavailing (emphasis supplied)."

(a) Equivalent to Specific Performance Action

The seller's action for the price (when buyer has not accepted the goods) is seller's remedial equivalent to the buyer's action for specific performance. (See § 5.6 supra). Just as specific performance is limited to cases in which the buyer

[*188*]

cannot cover, the seller's action for the price (when buyer has not accepted) is limited to cases in which a resale cannot be made. If seller is unable to resell the goods, UCC 2–709 allows him to push them off on the buyer and recover the price. This rule puts the seller in as good a position as he would have been in had the buyer not breached.

(b) Sellers Rights and Obligations with Respect to the Goods

Because a seller who sues for the price of withheld goods is, in effect, specifically enforcing the contract, he must be in a position to perform his part of the contract by being ready, willing and able to deliver the goods to the buyer once the price is paid or recovered. But a judgment against the buyer in the amount of the price does not necessarily mean that the seller will be able to collect it. The Code accordingly permits the seller to resell the withheld goods to enforce the judgment. Where the goods are sold to satisfy the judgment, the net proceeds of the resale must be credited to the buyer, and payment of the entire judgment entitles the buyer to any goods not resold. UCC 2–709(2).

EXAMPLE. S and B enter a contract for the sale of a "tailor made" mink coat of "petite size" for $10,000. B repudiates the contract, and S's efforts to resell the coat are, initially, unavailing. Consequently, S sues for the price, and obtains a judgment of $10,000. Prior to S's collecting the judgment, X offers to buy the coat from S for $7,500. S may sell the coat to X, and collect the balance of the judgment ($2500) from B.

§ 7.6 Recovery of Incidental but Not Consequential Damages, UCC 2–710

UCC 2–710 permits the aggrieved seller to recover *incidental* damages "includ[ing] any commercially reasonable charges, expenses or commissions incurred in stopping delivery, in the transportation, care, or custody of goods after the buyer's breach, in connection with return or resale of the goods or otherwise resulting from the breach." Unlike the aggrieved buyer, however, the aggrieved seller is *not* permitted to recover *consequential* damages. The reason for this disparity in treatment is as follows: When a *seller* breaches a contract, his failure to deliver conforming goods may result in the buyer's not being able to use those goods in other transactions from which he expected to make a profit. [See e. g. Example in § 1.1(d) supra]. In certain situations, UCC 2–715(2) permits buyer to recover those consequential damages from seller. [See § 5.5 supra]. However, when a buyer breaches a contract, the seller is usually "aggrieved" in one sense only—he is deprived of money. Neither the Code nor the common law permits the seller to prove that he intended to use that money in other transactions from which he could have made a profit (e. g. that he intended to use the money to purchase Lucky Jack Uranium stock which has since doubled in value). The reason that seller is not permitted to prove or recover these "consequential" damages is twofold: (1) Such damages can usually not be proved with "reasonable certainty," and (2) unlike goods, money is always fungible. If buyer's breach deprives the seller of needed money, seller can always borrow that money at the current interest rate. Therefore, seller will be fully compensated by recovering from buyer damages computed according to the statutory formulae above, plus incidental damages, together with interest at the current rate. This rule, of course, ignores one reality, i. e., not all aggrieved sellers can borrow the money of which they are deprived by virtue of buyer's breach.

§ 7.7   Sellers Rights with Respect to Unfinished Goods, UCC 2–704

This Code section provides that "where the goods are unfinished an aggrieved seller may in the exercise of reasonable commercial judgment for the purposes of avoiding loss and of effective realization *either complete the manufacture* and wholly identify the goods to the contract or *cease manufacture* and resell for scrap or salvage value or proceed in any other reasonable manner" [emphasis supplied]. Under this section, "the seller is given express power to complete manufacture or procurement of the goods for the contract unless the exercise of reasonable commercial judgment *as to the facts as they appear at the time he learns of the breach* makes it clear that such action will result in a material increase in damages." Official Comment #2. This statutory rule seems to be consistent with the general common law rule of mitigation of damages.

EXAMPLE 1. S, a volume manufacturer of Soundway pianos, enters into a contract with B, a dealer, for the manufacture and sale of ten Soundways at $6,000 each. S's total manufacturing costs are $5,000 per piano; and, therefore, the contract will yield a total profit of $10,000. B repudiates soon after manufacture has commenced and at a time when S has performed a very small amount of work under the contract. At the time of breach, S knows that the market for Soundways is drying up; and that if he completes manufacture, he will be able to sell the pianos for no more than $4000 each. In such a case it would be commercially *unreasonable* for S to complete manufacture. At the time of breach S knows that if he ceases manufacture, he can recover $10,000 in lost profits (See UCC 2–708(2), § 7.4 supra). S also knows that if he completes and resells, his statutory damages, based on the "contract price-resale price" differential, will be approximately $20,000. [See UCC 2–706, § 7.2 supra].

Therefore, since "the facts as they appear at the time he learns of the breach make it clear that [completing manufacture] will result in a material increase in damages," the exercise of reasonable commercial judgment dictates that S should "cease manufacture and resell for scrap or salvage value." If S exercises commercially *unreasonable* judgment and completes manufacture of the pianos, he will be entitled only to the recovery which he would have had if he had behaved reasonably, i. e. $10,000.

EXAMPLE 2. Same facts but at the time of B's breach S does not have reason to know that the market for Soundways is drying up. In fact, he has reason to believe that if he completes manufacture, he will be able to resell the pianos for at least $6000. In this case, it is commercially reasonable for S to complete manufacture of the goods and resell them, even if in so doing, his damages turn out to be higher than they would have been had the goods been left unfinished and sold for scrap.

§ 7.8 Sellers Rights Against the Insolvent Buyer, UCC 2–702(1)

UCC 2–702(1) provides: "Where the seller discovers the buyer to be insolvent he may refuse delivery except for cash including payment for all goods theretofore delivered under the contract, and stop delivery [of goods in the possession of a carrier or other bailee]."

CHAPTER 8

REMEDIES AVAILABLE TO SELLER AFTER BUYER HAS ACCEPTED THE GOODS

After the buyer has accepted the goods, the primary remedy available to the aggrieved seller is an action for the price under UCC 2-709. In some circumstances, however, the seller is, instead, entitled to reclaim the goods under either UCC 2-507 (2) or UCC 2-702(2).

§ 8.1 Action for the Price, UCC 2-709

In the preceding discussion of remedies available to seller when buyer defaults and has not accepted the goods, it was noted that an action for the price is a rather extraordinary remedy and is permitted only if seller was unable to resell the goods. However, when the buyer has already accepted the goods, different considerations apply. Indeed, an action for the price of goods accepted (plus incidental damages) is the primary remedy available to seller.

(a) "Goods Accepted"

"Goods accepted by the buyer . . . include only goods as to which there has been no justified revocation of acceptance (See § 6.2 supra), for such a revocation means that there has been a default by the seller which bars his rights under this section." UCC 2-709, Official Comment #5.

§ 8.2 Payment Due and Demanded on Delivery: Sellers Right to Reclaim, UCC 2-507(2)

This section provides that "where payment is due and demanded on the delivery to the buyer of goods . . ., his right as against the seller to retain or dispose of them is conditional upon his making the payment due." If he does not make the payment, the seller is entitled to reclaim the goods. This remedy is the seller's analogue to the buyer's right to revoke acceptance (See § 6.2 supra), and its utilization has the effect of giving the seller the pre-acceptance rather than post-acceptance remedies.

(a) Ten Day Limitation Period

Official Comment #3 to UCC 2-507(2) imposes a ten-day limitation on the seller's right to reclaim under this section. If seller does not reclaim the goods within ten days after buyer receives them, seller will be deemed to have waived his reclamation rights.

§ 8.3 Seller's Right to Reclaim Goods Upon Discovery of Buyer's Insolvency, UCC 2-702(2)

When goods have been delivered to an insolvent buyer, an action for the price is obviously an insufficient remedy. What the seller needs in such a case is the right to reclaim the goods. This right is provided by UCC 2-702(2) which provides that "where the seller discovers that the buyer has received goods on credit while insolvent he may claim the goods upon demand made within ten days after . . . receipt. . . ."

(a) Misrepresentation: Ten Day Period Inapplicable

"If misrepresentation of solvency has been made to the particular seller in writing within three months before delivery, the ten day limitation does not apply." UCC 2-702(2). A false financial statement, whether innocently or fraudulently made, is a common example of a written misrepresentation of solvency sufficient to render the ten day limitation period inapplicable.

(b) Exclusion of Other Remedies

Because the right of the seller to reclaim goods constitutes preferential treatment as against the insolvent buyer's other creditors, UCC 2-702(3) provides that "successful reclamation of goods excludes all other remedies with respect to them."

(c) Rights of Those Purchasing in Good Faith from Buyer

If the original buyer disposes of the goods to another buyer in the ordinary course of business or to any other good faith purchaser, the right of reclamation in the seller is cut off. UCC 2-703(3).

PART III

CONTRACTUAL CONTROL OVER REMEDY

INTRODUCTION

Part III differs from the preceding portions of this Nutshell in one material respect. The common law and equitable remedies explored in Part I, as well as the statutory remedies described in Part II, are generally awarded by a court when the contract itself does not provide for a remedy. It is not unusual, however, for the parties themselves to write into their contract certain provisions governing the remedy to be awarded in the event of breach. Such provisions, which comprise the subject matter of the present part of this work, are of two general types: (1) Liquidated Damages Clauses (Chapter 9); and (2) Contractual Modifications or Limitations of Remedy (Chapter 10).

CHAPTER 9

LIQUIDATED DAMAGES CLAUSES

Frequently, the parties to a contract will agree, as one of the terms of their agreement, that, in the event of a breach, the culpable party should pay a specified amount to the injured party. When a term of this type is included in the contract, it is called a "liquidated damages" provision. In contrast to the more usual post-breach approaches to assessing damages, a liquidated damages provision *anticipates* a breach, setting the amount to be recovered before any party fails in his obligations under the contract. Because the actual damages which will result from the potential breach are often unknowable at the time of contracting, liquidated damages represent the parties pre-estimate of the extent of probable damages. Often, this pre-estimate will, in hindsight, turn out to be an inaccurate forecast of the harm actually caused by the breach. The question which then must be faced is whether the liquidated damages provision is binding on the parties; or whether, instead, the court should invalidate the provision and make its own independent assessment of damages.

§ 9.1 Functions of Liquidated Damages Provisions

A liquidated damages clause may be designed to serve one of at least three distinct functions. First, the parties may wish to avoid a protracted dispute and/or trial on the issue of damages. To this end, they may provide for liquidated damages as a convenient method of determining the amount to be paid in the event of breach. That is, the parties may intend the provision to be a good-faith pre-estimate of the probable actual damages which will be suffered by the injured party. Second, the clause might serve the function of coercing a party to perform his obligation. Parties seeking to accomplish this goal will generally provide for a liquidated sum which is in excess of the probable actual damages which might result from breach. Such a sum will serve as a warning to the promisor that any default will be extremely expensive; hence, the mere presence of the sum will often compel performance by threatening punishment in the event of breach. A liquidated damages clause which is designed for this purpose will usually be invalidated on the ground that it actually is a "penalty." Third, a liquidated damages provision may be designed to diminish the amount of loss to be borne by a defaulting promisor. A clause which is designed for this purpose will fix a sum which is less than the anticipated amount of damages. Cases falling into this third category will not be discussed, as they seem to arise very infrequently.

[NOTE: When a promisor attempts to limit his liability, he usually does so not under a liquidated damages clause but instead under a provision which *limits the types of remedies* which will be available to the other party. Such provisions, called "contractual modifications or limitations of remedy" are the subject matter of Chapter 10].

§ 9.2 Liquidated Damages Distinguished from Penalties

The enforceability of any contractual stipulation of a fixed sum of damages will usually depend on the court's determination of whether or not the stipulation does, in fact, represent a good-faith attempt to pre-estimate the probable extent of injury resulting from a potential breach. If the court determines that the provision is, in fact, a good-faith pre-estimate, it will usually conclude that the clause is a "liquidated damages" provision, and hence enforceable. If, on the other hand, the court finds that the function of the clauses was to coerce the defaulting party to perform his obligation, the court will conclude that the provision is a "penalty" clause and hence unenforceable. It must be stressed, however, that the terms "liquidated damages clause" and "penalty clause" are conclusory. That is, they are labels that the court affixes *after* it has made a determination as to whether or not the stipulated sum represents a good-faith pre-estimate of potential damages.

§ 9.3 Words Used in Contract Not Determinative

Whether the contract itself refers to the stipulated sum as "liquidated damages" or as a "penalty" is not (or should not be) determinative of the court's conclusion as to the true nature of the provision. .   .   .   The policy underlying this reluctance to judge provisions at face value is understandable—if enforceability depended only upon the use of the correct written phrase, oppressive and coercive penalties could be effectively levied simply by calling them "liquidated damages." Conversely, valid liquidated damages provisions, mistakenly called "penalties" or "forfeitures," could be denied enforcement simply because of a slip-up in drafting. Most courts, therefore, take lightly the specific words used by the parties, and base their decisions instead upon whether the provision seems to be aimed at providing for compensation for potential losses or, instead, for punishment. Frequently, clearly labeled "liquidated damages" provisions have been held void as penalties, even when the parties have specifically stated that the sum is not to be construed as a penalty. Conversely, provisions referred to as "penalties" or "forfeitures" have been enforced as really providing for liquidated damages. Although a few courts have maintained that the mere use of the words "penalty" or "forfeit" is conclusive in rendering the clause unenforceable, the majority will simply not allow those words to dictate the result of the case. The following illustrations are all based on judicial decisions in which the courts refused to let the words used in the contract dictate the result.

EXAMPLE 1. ("Liquidated damages" = penalty). Theater owner A enters a contract with actor

B, under which A promises to pay B $200 for each performance in A's theater, and B promises to give 40 performances each summer, for three consecutive summers. The contract also contains a provision stipulating that if either party breaches the agreement in *any* way—e. g., B refuses to perform for one night or A defaults in payment for a performance or series of performances—the breaching party must pay the other $5,000 as "liquidated damages." B breaches by refusing to give the last three performances of the final season. A's attempt to enforce the "liquidated damages" provision will probably fail. The $5,000 sum will probably be deemed to be a penalty because it does not seem to represent a genuine attempt to provide for compensation for each of the many greater and lesser types of injury that could have been caused by various major or minor breaches of the contract. Regardless of how many performances B refuses to give, his liability will be the same; hence the sum is not a reasonable pre-estimate of potential damages [see § 9.5(b) infra].

EXAMPLE 2. ("Penalty" = liquidated damages). The government contracted with Manufacturer to supply gun carriages. Haste was extremely important to the government, and it had therefore passed up lower bids on the gun carriages because Manufacturer had promised the fastest delivery. Government and Manufacturer agreed that for each day a given delivery of the gun carriages was delayed, a "penalty" of $35 would be imposed on Manufacturer, payable to Government. This sum was reached by a computation based on the average difference in price between Manufacturer and cheaper, but slower, suppliers. Manufacturer delayed the delivery of some of the gun carriages. In the landmark Supreme Court decision of *U. S. v. Bethlehem Steel Co.*, 205 U.S. 105 (1907), the $35 per day "penalty" was enforced as liquidated damages because it seemed to be a genuine attempt to compensate the Government, by means of a reasonable formula, for the losses which it had sustained by paying a higher price for a speedy delivery which it had not received.

EXAMPLE 3. ("Forfeit" = liquidated damages). Plumber C sells her business to Plumber D for $10,000. D immediately pays $8,500 to C. The two plumbers agree that the remaining $1,500 will become due and payable after one year, as long as C does not set up another business within the same town during that time. Otherwise, C will "forfeit" the $1,500 to D. Six months after the initial transaction, C sets up a competing business across the street from D. D might be able to retain the $1,500 in this case, even though the term "forfeit" was used. The fact that the actual damages suffered by D when C breaches the contract cannot be measured with certainty (see § 9.5 (a), infra) indicates that reasonable compensation was the function of the provision.

[*203*]

§ 9.4 Actual (Subjective) Intent of Parties Usually Not Determinative

As is discussed in the preceding subsection, the *expressed* intent of the parties, i. e. their use of the words "liquidated damages," "penalty," or "forfeit," does not determine the enforceability of the sum which is stipulated in the contract. Many courts have stated, however, that while the parties' *expressed* intent is not controlling, their actual, subjective intent is an important factor to be considered. But, in reality, if a court refuses to give weight to the words used in the contract, then there simply is no way to ascertain the parties' subjective intent. Their pleadings and testimony will generally be in conflict; one party will claim that the stipulated sum was a genuine attempt to pre-estimate damages, while the other will allege that the clause was inserted to coerce compliance by penalizing potential breach. This conflict belies the existence of a uniform intention, formulated jointly by the parties at the contract's inception —or at least the existence of a *provable* intention. Thus, as Professor Corbin has noted, references by a court to the intention of the parties is usually more conclusory than determinative. In other words, the court will actually apply *objective* tests (see § 9.5 infra), and if it concludes that the provision is enforceable, the parties will be found to have "intended" liquidated damages. But, when enforcement is denied, denial will often be based on a "finding" (actually inferred from objective factors) that the parties "intended" to provide for a penalty.

EXAMPLE.   Merchant A and Merchant B were partners.   A bought out B's interest in the partnership in consideration of which B agreed not to set up a similar business in the same town for a period of three years.   The contract provided that if B breached the agreement, a sum of $1,000 was to be collected by A as liquidated damages.   B breached.   In determining whether the sum was a penalty or, instead, liquidated damages, the court found the "real question . . .   to be, not what the parties *intended*, but whether the sum is, *in fact*, in the nature of a penalty; and this is to be determined by the magnitude of the sum, in connection with the subject matter, and not at all by the words or the understanding of the parties. . . .   It must, therefore, . . .   be very obvious that the actual intention of the parties . . .   is wholly immaterial."   The court determined the sum to be enforceable as a liquidated damages provision because A's damages were "not only uncertain in nature, but impossible to be exhibited in proof," thus applying the objective test set forth in subsection 9.5(a) infra.

§ 9.5   Objective Factors Determinative

Regardless of whether or not a court attempts to reconstruct the intention of the parties, it will usually adopt some form of the following two-prong objective test to determine whether a given provision is enforceable as a liquidated damages clause, or invalid as a penalty. First, the potential damages must be uncertain or difficult to estimate. Second, the stipulated sum must be a reasonable pre-estimate of the probable damages.

(a) Damages Uncertain or Difficult to Estimate

If, at the time of contracting, it appears that potential damages are difficult to estimate, the parties may be concerned that, should a breach occur, it will necessitate a protracted dispute and/or trial on the issue of the amount of damages. To avoid this result, the parties may provide for a stipulated sum as a convenient method of determining the amount to be paid in the event of breach. That stipulated sum will usually be upheld if and only if it appears to represent a good-faith pre-estimate of damages which are uncertain or difficult to pre-estimate. If the potential damages are not uncertain in amount, then there is no need for a liquidated damages clause because the court will be able to calculate damages easily by applying the appropriate formula.

EXAMPLE 1. The XYZ Company specializes in counseling businesses on matters of employee efficiency. Each "efficiency expert" hired by XYZ receives extensive training, learning the secrets of the XYZ "observe and modify" technique. Defendant was hired by XYZ and was schooled in the technique in preparation for his being sent out to aid XYZ's clients. Defendant's employment contract included the following clause: "Any fully-trained employee who leaves the company promises not to divulge the XYZ technique to our competitors nor to use the technique for a period of one year from the end of his employment. Anyone violating this promise shall pay to XYZ Company the sum of $5,000 as liquidated damages." Immediately after his training period was completed, Defendant resigned from the XYZ Company and began operating as a "free-lance" efficiency expert, using the XYZ technique. Assuming that $5,000 is a reasonable sum (see discussion of "reasonableness" test, infra), the XYZ Company can probably enforce its damages provision. Defendant's use of privileged "trade secrets," in violation of his employment contract, will probably damage the XYZ Company; yet the damages will be impossible to measure. (NOTE: Since the contract clause in a non-competition covenant, XYZ Company could, at its option, seek specific performance [See § 4.2(a) supra] instead of liquidated damages. The court will not, however, grant both remedies; to do so would result in double recovery for XYZ).

EXAMPLE 2. Vendor sells a parcel of land, L, to Vendee. In addition to paying the contract price, Vendee promises to move a house, which stands partially on lot L and partially on lot M, off of lot L, so that it rests entirely upon lot M. Vendor had previously inquired at various house-moving companies, and had found that, at most, the job would cost $1,000. The contract, however, contains a provision for a sum of $5,000 to be paid to Vendor by Vendee as "liquidated damages" and not a "penalty" if Vendee does not perform as promised. Vendee pays the purchase price, but refuses to move the house. When Vendor brings an action to enforce the liquidated damages provision, she will probably not succeed. Because Vendor's damages are certain in amount, it seems clear that the $5,000 was intended to penalize nonperformance, not to remedy Vendor's potential losses. Thus, the court will invalidate the liquidated damages clause and will award actual damages of $1,000.

Uncertainty of Damages under the Uniform Commercial Code; UCC 2–718(1)

The Uniform Commercial Code tracks the common law principle that potential damages must be uncertain or difficult to estimate in order for the clause to be enforceable. UCC 2–718(1) provides that "Damages for breach by either party may be liquidated in the agreement but only at an amount which is reasonable in light of [1] the anticipated or actual harm caused by the breach, [2] the difficulties of proof of loss, and [3] the inconvenience or nonfeasibility of otherwise obtaining an adequate remedy." Parts [2] and [3] of this subsection—"difficulties of proof of loss" and "inconvenience or nonfeasibility of otherwise obtaining an adequate remedy" are simply another way of stating the "uncertainty of damages" principle. For, if the amount of damages is certain and/or easy to estimate, then proof of loss will not be difficult and adequate remedies will be feasible under the Buyers and Sellers Remedies sections of the UCC. (See Chapters 5 through 8 supra).

(b) Reasonableness in Light of Anticipated or Actual Harm

The second prerequisite to the enforceability of a liquidated damages clause is that the stipulated sum must be "reasonable." The question which arises is whether reasonableness of the agreed amount is to be judged only in light of the loss which is *anticipated* at the time of contracting or may reasonableness also be determined in light of the damages which *actually* occur.

Common Law Rule: Reasonableness Usually Judged in Light of Anticipated Harm

The common law rule in a majority of jurisdictions was (and is) that the reasonableness of the liquidated damages clause is to be judged solely in light of the loss which is anticipated at the time of contract formation. The damages which *actually* occur are irrelevant. Indeed, the major purpose of a liquidated damages clause is to avoid the necessity of having to ascertain the amount of damages which were actually caused by the breach. A few courts, however, have expressly considered actual losses.

EXAMPLE 1. Same facts as in a previous Example. The XYZ Company specializes in counseling businesses on matters of employee efficiency. Each "efficiency expert" hired by XYZ receives extensive training, learning the secrets of the XYZ "observe and modify" technique. Defendant was hired by XYZ and was schooled in the technique, in preparation for his being sent out to aid XYZ's clients. Defendant's employment contract included the following clause: "Any fully trained employee who leaves the company promises not to divulge the XYZ technique to our competitors nor to use the technique for a period of one year from the end of his employment. Anyone violating this promise shall pay to the XYZ Company $5,000 as liquidated damages." Immediately after his training period was completed, Defendant resigned from the XYZ Company and began operating as a freelance efficiency expert, using the XYZ technique. XYZ brings suit to enforce the liquidated damages provision. At trial, Defendant attempts to prove that since he has not stolen any clients or potential clients from XYZ, there is no *actual* damage to the Company. Under the majority rule, X will not be able to present his proof. The reasonableness of the five thousand dollar sum will be judged in light of the potential losses which were anticipated at the time of contracting, not in light of any losses which did or did not actually occur. In some jurisdictions, however, the courts will admit the evidence of *actual* losses (or lack thereof) and will invalidate initially reasonable clauses in light of the hindsight of what did, in fact, occur.

EXAMPLE 2. Same facts as in a previous example. Theater owner A enters a contract with Actor B, under which A promises to pay B two hundred dollars for each performance in A's theater, and B promises to give 40 performances each summer for three consecutive summers. The contract also contains a provision stipulating that if either party breaches the agreement in any way, e.g. B refuses to perform for one night or A defaults in payment for a performance or series of performances—the breaching party must pay the other $5,000 as liquidated damages. B breaches by refusing to give the last three performances of the final season. An attempt by A to enforce the liquidated damages provision will probably fail. But, under the majority rule, the reasonableness of the sum will not be judged in light of any harm or lack of harm actually resulting from B's breach. The five thousand dollar sum will be deemed to be a penalty because it was not *at the time of contract formation* a genuine attempt to provide compensation for the lesser and greater types of injury that could be caused by various major or minor breaches of the contract. A liquidated damages clause which fixes a flat sum for both major and minor breaches of the contract will usually not be considered to be a reasonable pre-estimate of anticipated damages.

UCC 2–718(1): Reasonableness Judged in Light of Anticipated or Actual Harm

Under UCC 2–718(1) the liquidated damages provision must be "reasonable in the light of the *anticipated or actual* harm caused by the breach." The more widely accepted interpretation of this section is that the clause is enforceable if plaintiff can demonstrate that the stipulated sum is proportionate to *either* anticipated *or* actual harm. But, under an alternative interpretation adopted by some courts, plaintiff must show that the amount is proportionate to both the anticipated *and* actual harm. Under this latter interpretation, defendant can have the clause invalidated by demonstrating that the stipulated sum is disproportionate to either anticipated *or* actual damages. In practice, this latter interpretation allows defendant to defeat the liquidated damages clause by proving that the actual damages were less than the stipulated sum, even though the stipulated sum was reasonable at the time of contracting.

EXAMPLE. R, a restaurant owner who has recently acquired a liquor license, enters into a contract with D distillery company for the sale by D to R of 1,000 quarts of Licorice brandy, a newly marketed, popular drink, for five dollars a quart or $5,000. The purchase price is to be paid on delivery. At the time of contracting, D is the only manufacturer of Licorice brandy, and both parties assume that a breach by D will damage R. However, the amount of damages is difficult to estimate because R has not previously sold liquor on his premises and also it is not known whether the popularity of Licorice brandy will endure. The parties, in a genuine attempt to pre-estimate damages, provide that if D fails to deliver, he will pay $7,000 in liquidated damages. On the date set for delivery, D repudiates. However, by that time, there is an alternative source of Licorice brandy on the market and R is able to cover immediately for $6.50 per quart or $6,500. R does cover, and then brings suit against D for $7,000, the liquidated sum stipulated in the contract. D argues that since R was able to cover, his actual damages, measured by the contract price-cover price differential (see § 5.2 supra) or $1,500 should be the limit on recovery. Under the more widely accepted interpretation of UCC 2–718(1), the $7,000 clause is enforceable because R will be able to demonstrate that at the time of contracting the $7,000 sum was proportionate to *anticipated* potential lost profits. Under the alternative interpretation, however, defendant can have the clause invalidated by showing that the actual damages ($1,500) are less than the stipulated sum.

§ 9.6 Statutory Imposition of Liquidated Damages under UCC 2–718(2)(b)

The preceding portions of this Chapter on liquidated damages are applicable only when the contract itself contains a liquidated damages provision. Because the term "liquidated damages" means, in essence, "agreed-upon damages" one would assume that neither the common law nor the Uniform Commercial Code would, in the absence of a contract provision, impose such damages on either party. While this is generally true, there is one exception—the *statutory* imposition of liquidated damages under UCC 2–718(2)(b). That subsection provides that "Where the seller justifiably withholds delivery of goods because of the buyer's breach, the buyer is entitled to restitution of any amount by which the sum of his payments exceeds . . . [in the absence of a contractual liquidated damages provision] twenty percent of the value of the total performance for which the buyer is obligated under the contract or $500, whichever is smaller. . . ."

(a) Applicable Only When Buyer Is Defaulting Party

UCC 2–718(2)(b) applies only when a buyer, who has made part or full payment, defaults prior to delivery of the goods. In such a case the aggrieved seller is permitted to withhold delivery and retain, as *statutorily imposed liquidated damages*,

20% of the purchase price, but not exceeding $500. The rule is a special exception to the general principle which refuses to recognize penalties or forfeitures. "No distinction is made between cases in which the [buyer's] payment is to be applied on the price and those in which it is intended as security for performance. [The] subsection . . . is applicable to any deposit or down or part payment." UCC 2–718, Official Comment #2.

There is no analogous UCC section which statutorily imposes liquidated damages on a breaching seller who delivers part of the goods and then repudiates the contract. In such cases, the aggrieved buyer cannot recover or retain anything absent a showing of *actual* damages.

EXAMPLE 1.   S and B enter into a contract for the sale by S to B of 2,000 Yo-Balls for $2,000. B pays $1,000 down, and then repudiates the contract prior to delivery of the goods. S immediately resells the Yo-Balls to X for $2,500. B sues S for return of his down payment, arguing that since S was not injured by B's breach (he in fact made an additional profit from the sale to X), to allow S to retain any or all of the down payment would amount to an invalid forfeiture or penalty against B. B's argument will fail. B is entitled to restitution only of the amount by which the sum of his payments [in this case $1,000] exceeds 20% of the purchase price [20% of $2,000 = $400]. Thus B may recover $600, and must "forfeit" $400 to S.

EXAMPLE 2.   S and B enter into a contract for the sale of S to B of 2,000 Yo-Balls for $2,000. S delivers only 1,000 Yo-Balls and then repudiates the remainder of the contract prior to B's having made any payment.   There is no UCC provision which permits B to retain some of the goods *without paying for them* as statutory liquidated damages resulting from S's breach.   B may, of course, recover *actual* damages if he can prove them.

CHAPTER 10

CONTRACTUAL MODIFICATION OR LIMITATION OF REMEDY UNDER UCC 2-719

INTRODUCTION

The preceding Chapter discusses principles to be applied when one of the parties attempts to *expand his own remedies* beyond those ordinarily recoverable at common law or under the UCC. In contrast, the instant Chapter deals with principles governing contractual provisions under which one of the parties has attempted to *limit or modify the other party's remedial rights*. The typical situation is that of a seller who, in addition to or in lieu of providing for a disclaimer of warranties (a topic which is beyond the scope of this text), attempts to restrict the remedies available to the buyer. Cases of this type occur with great frequency and are governed by UCC 2-719. The discussion in this Chapter is limited to a discussion of a *seller's* attempts to limit the remedies available to a *buyer*. It must be stressed however, that 2-719 applies equally to the rare case in which a buyer attempts to constrict the seller's remedies. Moreover, contractual limitations of remedies can and do occur in contexts outside the scope of the

UCC—for example, when a landlord attempts to restrict the remedies available to a tenant. Even though such cases are not directly governed by the Code, UCC 2–719 can be applied by analogy, as the common law principles applicable to contractual limitations of remedy are very similar to those which are embodied in that Code provision.

§ 10.1   Limitation of Remedies under 2–719(1)

UCC 2–719(1)(a) provides:

"Subject to the provisions of subsections (2) and (3) of this section and of the preceding section on liquidation and limitation of damages, (a) the agreement may provide for remedies in addition to or in substitution for those provided in this Article and may limit or alter the measure of damages recoverable under this Article as by limiting the buyer's remedies to return of the goods and repayment of the price or to repair and replacement of nonconforming goods or parts;"

The opening sentence of Official Comment #1 describes the "freedom of contract" policy underlying the provision:

"Under this section parties are left free to shape their remedies to their particular requirements and reasonable agreements limiting or modifying remedies are to be given effect."

[*218*]

The freedom granted to a seller under 2–719 does, however, have its limits. The text of subsection (1), as well as the Official Comments and case law, make it clear that not all contractual limitations on remedies will be upheld. A buyer seeking judicial invalidation of such a limitation has, under subsection (1), at least two routes open to him: (a) He can argue that the limitation is unreasonable and hence unconscionable; and/or (b) He can argue that the parties did not intend the limited remedy to be the only remedy available to buyer.

(a) Unconscionability

The opening paragraph of Comment #1 provides that *"reasonable* agreements limiting or modifying remedies are to be given effect." (emphasis supplied). Moreover, the second paragraph of that Comment explicitly states that a provision which gives the buyer less than a "fair quantum of remedy" will be stricken as unconscionable:

> "[I]t is of the very essence of a sales contract that at least minimum adequate remedies be available. If the parties intend to conclude a contract for sale within this Article they must accept the legal consequence that there be at least a fair quantum of remedy for breach of the obligation or duties outlined in the contract. *Thus any clause purporting to modify*

or limit the remedial provisions of this Article in an unconscionable manner is subject to deletion and in that event the remedies made available by this Article are applicable as if the stricken clause had never existed. [emphasis supplied].

The cases which have interpreted the "unconscionability" component of subsection (1) have focused on the same factors as are considered when making a determination of "unconscionability" under the Code's general "unconscionability" provision, UCC 2–302. [See Chapter 14 infra]. For example, sharp practices on the part of the seller and disparity of expertise or bargaining power between the parties are two elements which are frequently considered.

EXAMPLE. Seller, a used car dealer, sold a used foreign-made car to buyer, a consumer. The agreement contained a provision (in small print) which limited the buyer's remedy to repair and replacement of defective parts and specifically provided that that remedy was the "sole and exclusive" remedy available to buyer. The car's brakes were defective, and seller was not able to replace them as the manufacturer of the car was no longer in business. Seller did repair the brakes, but buyer, who was not entirely satisfied with the results, wanted to return the car and recover the purchase price. In invalidating the "repair and replacement" limitation, the court held that the seller's conduct (i. e. burying the clause in a maze of fine print) rendered the clause unconscionable; and, in the alternative, that the clause might not have even been part of the parties' original agreement. The court stressed that a contractual limitation on remedies must be part of the parties' bargain *in fact*. In this case, the clause was inconspicuous (i. e. buried in small print and not brought to the buyer's attention). Thus, the seller could not reasonably expect that the buyer understood that his remedies were being limited to repair and replacement and that he would not be permitted to return a defective vehicle. For that reason, the limitation provision could not be considered to be part of the parties' agreement. The court also stressed the disparity in expertise and bargaining power on the part of the parties and indicated that it would have been less likely to strike the clause if both parties had been car dealers. [NOTE: This case did not involve the unconscionability component of subsection (3) of 2–719 (discussed infra) as the buyer was not seeking consequential damages].

(b) Remedy Not Intended to be Exclusive

A second route available to a buyer seeking freedom from a contractual limitation on remedy is to argue that the remedy stipulated was not intended to be the only remedy available to him. A pre-

sumption to this effect is contained in the text of
2–719(1)(b). That subsection provides that:

> "resort to a remedy as provided is optional
> unless the remedy is expressly agreed to be
> exclusive, in which case it is the sole remedy."

Official Comment #2 states that:

> "Subsection (1)(b) creates a presumption that
> clauses prescribing remedies are cumulative
> rather than exclusive. If the parties intend
> the term to describe the sole remedy under the
> contract, this must be clearly expressed."

Some judicial interpretations of 2–719(1)(b), particularly in cases involving consumer transactions,
make it clear that if the seller intends the stipulated remedy to be exclusive, he must express that
intention in extraordinarily precise language.

EXAMPLE. Buyer purchased a used car from
seller, a dealer, under a contract which limited
seller's "liability" to repair and replacement of defective parts. The contract specifically provided
that the repair and replacement provision was "expressly in lieu of any other liability on the part of
the seller." The car was defective, and buyer
sought to return it and recover the purchase price.
In holding that the buyer was not limited to the
repair and replacement provision, the court reasoned that the contract limited only the seller's *liability* and did not specifically state that the *remedy*
of repair and replacement was exclusive. Since

the contractual language was insufficient for purposes of 2–719(1)(b), buyer could treat the "repair and replacement" provision as optional, and could resort to other statutory remedies such as return of the goods and recovery of the purchase price.

Such strained interpretations of 2–719(1)(b) are more common in transactions involving consumers than in cases in which both parties are businessmen. Nevertheless, in either type of transaction, a seller who desires to restrict the buyer's remedies should do so in very specific and precise terms. In cases of the type described in the preceding example, Professors White and Summers have suggested the following language:

> "The parties agree that the buyer's sole and exclusive remedy against the seller shall be for the repair or replacement of defective parts as provided herein. The buyer agrees that no other remedy (including, but not limited to, incidental or consequential damages for lost profits, lost sales, injury to person or property, or any other incidental or consequential loss) shall be available to him."

It should be noted that the desirability (from the seller's standpoint) of including the phrase "injury to person" in the limitation provision is debatable. For, under 2–719(3) [See § 10.3 infra], limitation of consequential damages for personal injury in the

case of consumer goods is prima facie unconscionable. Thus, White and Summers have added
to their suggested language the following caveat:
"The seller's chances of [overcoming the presumption of unconscionability] .   .   .   should be
weighed against the possibility that a court would
strike the entire limitation of remedy clause because of the single unconscionable term." It is
this author's opinion that, in cases involving exclusion of consequential damages for personal injury, the likelihood of overcoming the presumption
of unconscionability is very slight. Therefore, a
seller wishing to draft a limitation provision which
will be sufficient for purposes of 2–719(1)(b) would
be well-advised to adopt the White-Summers for-
mulation, but to omit the language excluding remedies for "injury to person."

§ 10.2 Failure of Essential Purpose under 2–719 (2)

UCC 2–719(2) provides: "Where circumstances
cause an exclusive or limited remedy to fail of its
essential purpose, remedy may be had as provided
in this Act."

This subsection is certainly one of the most poorly drafted sentences in Article Two. As Professor
Nordstrom has pointed out:

> "Remedies do not have 'purposes'—let alone an
> essential purpose. People have purposes in en-
> tering into agreements, but these purposes

[*224*]

may differ depending upon whether the buyer or seller is being considered. If the seller prepared the form which severely limits any remedy which the buyer has in the event of default, it is not unreasonable to believe that the seller's 'purpose' was exactly that which is spelled out in the clause. His purpose was that of selling goods and limiting liability for defects later discovered. The buyer's purpose may well have been different; he may have wanted the goods and full remedies in the event of breach. To talk about a purpose—as the Code does—confuses the test which the court should apply in determining whether to enforce the limitation-of-remedies clause."

Only by engrafting the Official Comments onto the text of Subsection (2) can one discern what is meant by "fail[ure] of . . . essential purpose." Comment #1 provides:

"Where an apparently fair and reasonable clause *because of circumstances* fails in its essential purpose or *operates to deprive either party of the substantial value of the bargain*, it must give way to the general remedy provisions of this Article." [emphasis supplied].

When properly applied, subsection (2) is not concerned with limitation clauses which were unreasonable and/or unconscionable at their inception. Such clauses would, instead, be struck under the unconscionability concept inherent in subsection (1) [See § 10.1(a) supra] and/or the conscionability requirement contained in subsection (3) [See § 10.3 infra]. Rather, subsection (2) is addressed to clauses which were fair and reasonable at the outset but, because of circumstances not contemplated by the parties, operate in a manner which will deprive one of the parties of the substantial value of his bargain. [See EXAMPLE 1 below]. Some courts, however, have mis-applied subsection (2) and have used that provision to invalidate contractual provisions which were oppressive or unreasonable as drafted. [See EXAMPLE 2 below].

EXAMPLE 1. Buyer purchases a sailboat from seller under a contract which limits buyer's remedies to repair or replacement of defective parts. Such a limitation is fair and reasonable in its inception and will usually operate in a fair and reasonable manner. For example, if there is a defect in the rudder, the rudder can be repaired or a new one installed. Suppose, however, the defective rudder malfunctions while the boat is in use, causing the boat to collide with a large yacht. As a result, the sailboat sinks, is totally destroyed, and damages the yacht with which it collided. In such a case, it is not the limitation clause itself which is unreasonable, but rather the intervening event (the collision) which has caused the buyer to be deprived of more than the value of her bargain.

The repair and replacement remedy is now no remedy at all. Buyer is without a boat and has suffered consequential losses in that she will face liability to the owner of the yacht. The limitation clause might be held to have "failed its essential purpose"; if so, buyer may recover under the other remedial provisions of Article 2.

EXAMPLE 2. *Wilson Trading Corp. v. David Ferguson, Ltd.*, 23 N.Y.2d 398, 297 N.Y.S.2d 108, 244 N.E.2d 685 (1968), illustrates a misapplication of UCC 2–719(2). In that case, buyer purchased yarn under a contract which provided that all claims must be made within ten days after receipt of shipment. Buyer, a sweater manufacturer, claimed that the yarn contained latent defects which could not be discovered within the ten day period. The court held, *inter alia*, that if buyer's allegation was true, then the contractual limitation on remedy "failed of its essential purpose." In so holding, the court seems to have misapplied 2–719 (2). It is not the *circumstances* which deprived the buyer of the substantial value of his bargain. Instead, the contractual limitation period was probably unreasonable as drafted in that it deprived buyer of *all* remedies for any defects which could not be discovered within the ten-day period. Thus, if buyer's allegations were true (i. e. there were latent defects which could not be discovered within ten days), then the contractual limitation should have been struck under 2–719(1),

2–719(3) and/or 2–302 [See Chapter 14 infra] all of which deal with inherently unconscionable terms.

(a) Consequences of Invalidation

If a limitation clause is struck on the ground of "failure of essential purpose", then, under subsection (2), "remedy may be had as provided in this Act." According to Official Comment #1, this last clause means that if the limited remedy fails, then it "give[s] way to the general remedy provisions of this Article." It is not clear, however, whether this allows the buyer to resort to the *full range* of remedies available under the Code or whether, instead, the buyer will be able to recover only what he could have recovered if the limited remedy had not "failed of its essential purpose." This is an issue on which there is a split of authority.

EXAMPLE. Suppose in the sailboat example (EXAMPLE 1 above) the contract not only limits buyer's remedies to repair or replacement of defective parts but also expressly provides that buyer cannot recover consequential damages. While the sailboat is in use, the rudder malfunctions, causing the boat to collide with a large yacht. As a result, the sailboat is totally destroyed and also has damaged the yacht with which it collided. The intervening event (the collision) may have caused the repair and replacement remedy to fail its essential purpose—to ensure the buyer of a sailboat free of defects. Suppose, however, that seller argues that the essential purpose of the limited remedy is twofold: First, to guarantee that buyer will have a non-defective sailboat; and second, to relieve seller from any responsibility (other than damage to the sailboat) which results from the vessel's malfunctioning. Thus, according to seller, because the repair and replacement remedy has failed, buyer is entitled to either return of the purchase price or a new sailboat, but *not* consequential damages (i. e. indemnification for damage caused to the yacht). Essentially seller's argument is that if the repair and replacement remedy had not failed (i. e. if the sailboat hadn't been destroyed and the rudder could have been repaired or replaced), then seller would not have been liable for consequential losses resulting from damage to the yacht. And, the argument continues, buyer should not be allowed to recover a larger amount of damages than she bargained for, i. e. more than she would have gotten if the limited remedy contained in the contract had not failed its essential purpose. Some courts have, in fact, adopted this position and, while invalidating a "repair and replacement" provision under subsection (2) have, at the same time, sustained a provision excluding consequential damages, particularly when that exclusion is contained in a "separate clause." Other courts have taken a contrary position, holding that under 2–719(2) and Official Comment #1, if a limitation on remedy fails, then the *entire* limitation fails. In that event, the aggrieved buyer is entitled to *all* Article 2 remedies, including consequential damages.

§ 10.3 Unconscionable Limitation on Consequential Damages under 2–719(3) and 2–302

The final requirement of 2–719 is that a provision which limits or excludes *consequential* damages must not be unconscionable. 2–719(3), in its entirety, provides:

> Consequential damages may be limited or excluded unless the limitation or exclusion is unconscionable. Limitation of consequential damages for injury to the person in case of consumer goods is prima facie unconscionable but limitation where the loss is commercial is not.

The concept of unconscionability, as explicitly incorporated into UCC 2–719(3), is discussed in Chapter 14, § 14.3(c), infra.

PART IV

REMEDIES FOR MISTAKE AND UNCONSCIONABILITY

INTRODUCTION

The preceding portions of this book have, with a few minor exceptions, dealt with remedies for *breach* of *enforceable* contracts. Often, however, a plaintiff or defendant will seek judicial relief *not* because the other party is in breach but, instead, because the contract is contaminated by some defect which, it is claimed, renders the contract (or one of its provisions) a nullity. These contractual contaminants fall into five categories: "fraud," "duress," "undue influence," "mistake" and "unconscionability."

It was originally this author's intention to devote the final part of this Nutshell to a brief discussion of all five of these topics. However, an informal poll of a statistically insignificant number of Contracts professors revealed that three categories of contractual contaminants—"fraud," "duress" and "undue influence" are either not covered in the basic Contracts course or else, when they are discussed, are given scant attention. The explanation usually given for this phenomenon is that (1) Fraud and Undue Influence are given extensive coverage in other courses; and (2) Duress, to the

[*231*]

extent that it involves a "contract made at gun-point" occurs with extreme infrequency in modern contract law. Instead, the modern "duress" cases usually involve the elements of ignorance, poverty, sharp dealing and/or inequality of bargaining power, and thus can be subsumed within the topic of unconscionability.

In contrast, the last two categories of contractual contaminants—mistake and unconscionability—are given coverage in most basic Contracts courses. These topics are approached not only in terms of their substantive elements but also with an eye towards their remedial implications. Because it is the purpose of this Nutshell to track, as closely as possible, the remedies issues covered in the first-year Contracts course, the final portion of this book will be devoted to a discussion of the remedial ramifications of "Mistake" and "Unconscionability."

CHAPTER 11

MISTAKE IN THE FORMATION OF AN AGREEMENT—THE RECISSION AND RESTITUTION REMEDIES

INTRODUCTION

Whenever a party to a contract seeks relief on the grounds that a mistake has been made, the first question which must be asked is: at what stage in the contractual relationship did the alleged mistake occur? The answer to this question will usually determine the choice of remedies, if any, which will be available to the aggrieved party.

In general, there are three points in a contractual relationship at which a mistake can occur: (1) During the *formation* of the contract; (2) During the writing-out, or *integration*, of the contract; and (3) During the *performance* of obligations under the contract. Because the choice of available remedies differs markedly at each of these three contractual stages, each stage will be discussed in a separate chapter.

The most frequently occurring allegation of contractual mistake is that the contract was *formed* on the basis of a mistaken assumption. When relief is sought on this ground, an inquiry must first be made as to the *type* of mistake which has been alleged.

[*233*]

For, there are certain types of formation "mistakes" for which the law provides *no* remedy, and others for which the law provides relief only rarely. Thus, this Chapter on "Mistakes in Contract Formation" is divided into two major sections. Section 11.1 is a discussion of the types of mistake which might occur during contract formation (i.e. the substantive framework upon which the remedial format is based); Section 11.2 is a discussion and analysis of the remedies available for mistakes which are made at this initial stage of the contract.

§ 11.1 Substantive Framework—Types of Mistake Which Might Occur in the Formation of a Contract

In the law of contract formation, a mistake is a belief which is not in accord with the facts. It is often stated that a party alleging mistake will be entitled to relief if and only if he can establish a *mutual mistake of existing material fact(s)*.

EXAMPLE. On Friday morning, vendor and vendee enter into a contract for the sale of vendor's lake-front cabin for $100,000. Unbeknownst to the parties, the cabin was totally destroyed by fire on Thursday evening. Since the contract was formed on the basis of a mutual belief (i. e. both parties believed that the cabin was in existence), and that belief is not in accord with the existing material facts, both parties will be relieved of their obligations under the contract.

[234]

In order to understand the concept of *mutual mistake of existing material fact*, it is necessary to contrast it with other types of mistake which might occur in a contractual relationship.

(a) Mistake of Existing Fact as Opposed to Misjudgment About the Future

Often, two parties will enter a contract with two different sets of expectations regarding future occurrences. For example, in a contract for the sale of grain, the buyer may expect that the market price for grain will increase, while the seller may expect it to decline. In such cases, each party is taking the risk that events might not turn out in accordance with his own predictions. When one party's prediction is later revealed to have been a misjudgment, it seems obvious that contractual relief should not be granted on grounds of "mistake." Moreover, even if it can be shown that at the time of contracting, *both* parties had erroneous expectations regarding future events, there is still no mistake of existing fact, and hence no relief will be granted.

EXAMPLE. On February 1, S and B enter into a contract for the sale by S to B of several silver heirlooms for $5,000. S is to deliver the heirlooms and B is to pay for them on May 1. At the time of contracting, the market price of silver is advancing steadily, and B believes that on May 1, the silver heirlooms will be worth substantially more than $5,000. On February 10, however, the market for silver begins to decline rapidly, and on May 1, the heirlooms are worth only $3,500. B asks a court to "rescind" (undo) the contract on grounds of mistake. Relief will be denied. This will be true even if B can prove that at the time of contracting S also believed that the price of silver would continue to advance and that S had entered into the contract only because she needed the cash. In such a case, there will have been only a mutual misprediction of future events, not a mutual mistake of fact.

(b) Mistake of Fact as Opposed to "Conscious Ignorance" of the Facts

A party cannot make a "mistake of fact" unless he reasonably believes that he knows the existing facts, but his belief is at variance with reality. If, on the other hand, the party is aware that he is ignorant or uncertain as to the facts, but chooses to enter the contract in spite of his limited knowledge, he will not be granted relief on the basis that the facts turned out to be unfavorable to him. In such a case, because the party could have made a further investigation or refused to contract until the true facts were discovered, he will be said to have "assumed the risk" that the existing facts were not favorable to his interests.

Sometimes it will be clear that a case poses a problem of "conscious ignorance" as opposed to "mistake." (See EXAMPLE 1, below). In other situations, however, it will be very difficult to draw the line between these two states of mind. (See EXAMPLE 2, below). Yet, the distinction is a critical one because if the party was truly mistaken as to the facts, relief will be granted, but if he was "consciously ignorant" of those facts, no remedy will be available.

EXAMPLE 1. Vendor and vendee enter into a contract for the sale of Blackacre. Both parties know that oil has recently been discovered on an adjacent tract of land, but neither vendor nor vendee knows whether oil will be found on Blackacre. Because vendor knows or has reason to know of his own ignorance but nevertheless enters the contract in spite of his limited knowledge, he will not be allowed to rescind the contract if oil is later discovered. Likewise, vendee will not be entitled to relief if oil is not found on the property.

EXAMPLE 2. In the landmark case of *Sherwood v. Walker*, 66 Mich. 568, 33 N.W. 919 (1887), buyer and seller entered into a contract for the sale of a cow, "Rose 2d of Aberlone," for $80. Prior to the sale, seller told buyer that the cow was "probably barren and would not breed." Subsequently, seller learned that, far from being barren, Rose was actually with calf at the time of sale. Because a breeder cow was worth at least $750 (whereas the cow, if barren, would have been worth only $80), seller refused to deliver and sought to rescind the contract. The court permitted recission on the grounds that both parties had believed that the cow was barren, and that this mutual belief was not in accord with the existing facts. Thus, a true mutual mistake had occurred. There was a strong dissent which took the position that this was not a case of mistaken belief, but was, instead a case of conscious ignorance. Hence, no recission should have been allowed: "In this case neither party knew the actual quality and condition of this cow at the time of sale. .   .   .   As to the quality of the animal .   .   .   both parties were equally ignorant, and as to this each party took his chances." *Sherwood v. Walker* illustrates the difficulty in drawing the line between the two states of mind known as (1) mistake of existing fact (for which a remedy will be granted), and (2) conscious ignorance of existing fact (for which no relief will be granted).

(c) Mistake as Opposed to Ambiguity

In a true "mistake" case, the parties are holding beliefs which are not in accord with existing facts. There are some instances, however, where the parties beliefs *are* in accord with the existing facts but each party is contracting with reference to a different set of facts. Such cases are extremely rare, but when they do occur, the court will rescind the agreement on the grounds of "latent ambiguity."

EXAMPLE. In the famous case of *Raffles v. Wichelhaus*, 159 Eng.Rep. 375 (1864), buyer and seller entered into a contract for the sale of cotton to arrive from Bombay on a ship named Peerless. Unbeknownst to either party, there were two ships named Peerless from Bombay. The buyer had contracted with reference to the Peerless which was sailing in October, but the seller had contracted with respect to the Peerless which was sailing in December. Although the facts are unclear, it appears that the sailing date of the ship was important to the buyer. When the December Peerless arrived, buyer refused to accept the cotton and pay for it, and seller sued. The court held that because of the existence of a "latent ambiguity", no binding contract existed. While *Raffles v. Wichelhaus* is sometimes referred to as a "mistake" case, it should be noted that there really was no mistake because neither party held a belief which was at variance with existing facts. Instead, this was a true case of ambiguity, where each of the parties was contracting with reference to a different set of facts and each party was reasonable in his interpretation of the agreement.

Cases of true ambiguity are extremely rare. More frequent are situations in which one of the parties knows or has reason to know that the meaning which he has attached to the contract might be different from the meaning attached by the other party. In such a case, a court will not rescind the agreement but instead will uphold it and give it the meaning which was attached by the party who was unaware of the ambiguity.

EXAMPLE. Seller and buyer enter into a contract for the sale of 100 cases of wine from the Grapa Valley in California. There are two Grapa Valleys in California, and seller, who is aware of that fact, is contracting with respect to Grapa Valley North. Buyer, however, is aware of only one Grapa Valley—Grapa Valley South which is the better-known of the two, and generally produces a higher quality wine than does its Northern namesake. Thus, buyer neither knows nor has reason to know of the meaning attached by seller, whereas seller (because he knows that there are two Grapa Valleys) has reason to know of the meaning attached by buyer. In such a case, there is a binding contract between the parties in which seller has promised to deliver 100 cases of wine from Grapa Valley South.

(d) Mutual Mistake as Opposed to "Unilateral" Mistake

It is often stated that if a mistake is "unilateral" rather than "mutual," no relief will be available to the mistaken party. A "unilateral" mistake occurs whenever the negligence or oversight of *one party* is the primary cause of the mistake. The typical case is that of a contractor, who, when bidding on a construction contract, makes an error in computation and submits a bid which is lower than it would have been had the error not occurred. While the courts refer to this as a "unilateral" mistake, that term is actually a misnomer. While it is true that the negligence or oversight of *one party* (the bidder) is the *cause* of the mistake, it is usually the case that both the bidder and the recipient of the bid believe that the bid is the result of an accurate computation. Thus, both parties hold a belief which is at variance with existing facts, and the mistake is in fact, "mutual." Nevertheless, mistaken bidder cases are invariably referred to as instances of "unilateral" mistake; and it follows from that classification that recission of the contract is ordinarily not justified. The policy underlying this rule is that it is the purpose of contract law to fulfill the reasonable expectations of parties to a bargain. Thus, if a mistaken bidder, through his words or deeds, has created reasonable expectations on the part of the recipient of the bid, those expectations should not be thwarted merely because the bidder was in error.

EXAMPLE. City X invites and receives four bids on the construction of a proposed building. Contractor A bids $250,000; B bids $246,000; C bids $243,000; and D bids $240,000. A few days after D is awarded the contract, he discovers that he made an error in computation, and that his bid should have been $250,000 instead of $240,000.

D will not be permitted to rescind the agreement. His bid was not substantially lower than the other bids, and thus it was reasonable for the city to believe that the bid was the result of an accurate computation. The reasonable expectation of the City—that the building will be constructed for $240,000—should be fulfilled, either through D's performance or by his payment of damages.

Ironically, in cases involving mistaken bids, it is the *truly unilateral* mistake which *will* justify recission of the contract. That is, if the bidder believes that his bid is the result of an accurate computation, but the recipient of the bid knows or has reason to know that the bid was in error, then the mistake is truly unilateral in the sense that it is one-sided. Yet, it is this very situation—the one-sided mistake which is taken advantage of by the other party—which will justify relief for the mistaken party.

EXAMPLE. City X invites and receives four bids on the construction of a proposed building. Contractor A bids $250,000; B bids $246,000; C bids $243,000, and D bids $200,000. A few days after D is awarded the contract; he discovers that he had made an error in computation and that his bid should have been $250,000 instead of $200,000. D will probably be permitted to rescind the agreement. The disparity between D's bid and the other bids is sufficient to charge the City with notice of the probable error. Becase the City knows of or has reason to suspect the error, the City has no reasonable expectation that the building will be constructed for $200,000.

(e) Mistake of "Identity" or "Existence" of Subject Matter as Opposed to Mistake of "Value" or "Quality"

It is often stated that relief will be granted if and only if the mistake goes to the "identity" or "existence" of the subject matter; and that a mistake which is merely one of "value" or "quality" will not be a sufficient basis upon which to predicate recission. Occasionally, this principle is easily applied.

EXAMPLE. In the example at the beginning of this Chapter, both parties believed that the cabin was in existence when in fact it was not. In such a case, it is easy and sensible to apply a rule whereby the mistake, because it goes to the existence of the subject matter, ought to excuse the parties from their duties to perform. Suppose, on the other hand, that the cabin *was* in existence at the time of contracting, but that the parties had believed it to have a market value of $100,000 when, in fact, it had a market value of only $95,000. In such a case it would likewise be easy and sensible to apply a rule that the mistake, because it goes merely to the *value* of the subject matter, ought not to justify recission of the agreement.

Often, however, it will be impossible to place a mistake on one side or the other of the "line" created by the "existence-value" dichotomy. In such cases, there is room for considerable definitional manipulation of that dichotomy, and hence of the result.

EXAMPLE. In *Sherwood v. Walker*, the "pregnant cow" case discussed above, the court found that both parties shared the mutual belief that the cow was barren when, in fact, she was pregnant at the time of sale. This mistaken belief was, according to the court, sufficient to prevent the formation of a valid contract. In holding that there was no contract, the court said that it was applying the following rule: "If the thing actually delivered is different in substance from the thing bargained for, . . . then there is no contract; but if it be only a difference in some quality . . ., the contract remains binding." Then, surprisingly, the court concluded that "the mistake was not of the mere quality of the animal, but went to the very nature of the thing. . . . *the thing sold and bought had no existence*." (emphasis supplied). The court's statement, of course, was not true. The cow did in fact exist and she was the very cow which had been bargained for. It was simply a quality or characteristic (i. e. infertility) which did not exist, and that characteristic affected the *value* of the cow. Yet the court, in an astounding display of definitional gymnastics, stated that "the thing sold and bought had no existence," and thus concluded that the contract, too, had no existence. This case illustrates that the line between a "mistake in existence" and a "mistake in value" is often too illusive to draw, and might, therefore, be drawn arbitrarily or disingenuously. According to Professor Palmer, the *Sherwood* court erred by concentrating its attention on the definitional nature of the mistake instead of the extent to which the buyer would have been unjustly enriched had the contract not been rescinded. Palmer concludes that "it is probable that prevention of unjust enrichment influenced the decision, but the time has come to make this explicit."

§ 11.2 Remedies Available for Mistake In Formation of a Contract—Recission and Restitution

(a) Recission

Once it has been determined that mistake in formation is of the type for which relief should be granted, the court will usually order recission of the agreement. The consequences of such an order are generally two-fold: (1) The contractual rights and duties of each of the parties are terminated; (2) Each party obtains restitution of any performance he has rendered before the mistake was discovered.

Recissions Which Involve a Reinstatement of Prior Rights

Normally, a recission will simply put an end to each of the parties' rights and obligations under the agreement. In some cases, however, instead of terminating all rights and obligations, the recission will actually entail a reinstatement of rights and duties which the parties had prior to their entry into the "mistaken" contract. This occurs most frequently in situations involving settlement agreements which are set aside on the ground of mistaken assumptions.

EXAMPLE. Driver negligently operates his car and hits Pedestrian who suffers a head injury. Two weeks after the accident, Pedestrian's physician tells both Driver and Pedestrian that Pedestrian's injury was only temporary and superficial and that Pedestrian has fully recovered. On the basis of the physician's representation, Driver and Pedestrian sign a contract whereby the parties agree to settle the claim for $2,000 and Pedestrian agrees to release Driver from any further liability arising from the accident. Subsequently, it is discovered that Pedestrian's head injury is not only permanent but also so severe that he will not be able to work. Pedestrian asks the court to rescind the settlement agreement on the grounds that it had been formed on the basis of the physician's mistaken diagnosis. If the court orders recission, the result will be the reinstatement of Pedestrian's tort claim against Driver.

Recission as Both a Legal and Equitable Remedy

Historically, in both England and the United States, it was often stated that "the courts of common law have no power to set aside a contract on the ground of mistake." Therefore, relief through recission of an agreement could be obtained only in a court of equity. Today, under a procedural system in which law and equity have been merged, it will usually be unnecessary to consider whether the aggrieved party's request for recission is a request for equitable, as opposed to legal, relief. The distinction is still important, however, in cases in which one party desires to submit the issue of mistake to a jury. In such situations, there are some recent decisions to the effect that recission is both a legal and an equitable remedy. Thus, the issue of mistake can be submitted to the jury, but only if the plaintiff is seeking the kind of judgment which is otherwise within the traditional jurisdiction of a common law court.

EXAMPLE. In the immediately preceding EXAMPLE, Driver and Pedestrian entered into a settlement and release agreement which was formed on the basis of a physician's mis-diagnosis of the extent of Pedestrian's injuries. Suppose that, after discovering that his injuries are both permanent and severe, Pedestrian sues for damages based on the original tort. Driver defends on the basis of the release agreement, but Pedestrian counters with the allegation that that agreement was obtained because of a mistake and ought to be rescinded. Under the older cases, the plaintiff would be required to bring two lawsuits. First, the plaintiff would have to seek recission of the release agreement from a court of equity; and if that court ordered recission, then plaintiff would be free to bring a claim, based on the tort, in a court of law. Under modern law and procedure, however, the plaintiff is required to bring only one action; and the court can let the entire case go to the jury—not only on the issue of tort liability, but also on the issue of the alleged mistake underlying the release agreement. If the court believes that it would be too confusing for the jury to decide both issues simultaneously, the court can, in its discretion, order a separate trial on the issue of mistake in the release agreement before going to trial on the original tort claim.

The "Rule" Against Partial Recission

It is a cardinal "rule" that if a party is entitled to recission, the entire agreement must be set aside. A party will not be permitted to retain the benefits of some portions of the agreement while obtaining a court order that other portions be cancelled. There will be situations, however, in which a change of position by one or both of the parties before learning of the mistake will make recission *in toto* impossible; yet, to leave the plaintiff without a remedy will not only be unfair to her but will also result in unjust enrichment of the defendant. In such circumstances, several courts have indicated that they will not permit the rule against partial recission to operate as a bar to all relief, but will, instead, be flexible in devising a remedy that achieves substantial justice. Sometimes this can be accomplished by severing the contract into two or more "contracts", and rescinding the "contract" which the court has severed from the remainder. (See EXAMPLE 1, below). In other cases, it may be appropriate to allow the contract to stand but with an adjustment of the contract price, based on the notion that plaintiff is entitled to restitution of the amount by which she has been damaged due to the mistake. (See EXAMPLE 2, below).

EXAMPLE 1. Seller and Buyer enter into one written contract for the sale of two cows, Rose the First and Rose the Second, for a total price of $160. At the time of contracting, both parties believe that both cows are sterile; this belief is based primarily on the diagnosis of a veterinarian who has examined them prior to sale. The contract states that the $160 contract price represents the current value of the two cows on the beef market, $70 for Rose the First and $90 for Rose the Second, who weighs more. After Seller delivers both cows to buyer and receives payment of the purchase price, buyer re-sells Rose the First to a third party. Subsequently, it is discovered that Rose the Second is not only fertile but was actually with calf at the time of sale. A fertile cow, which can be used for dairy purposes, is worth $800. Seller seeks recission of the sale. In defense, Buyer argues that since he has already re-sold Rose the First, recission of the entire contract is not possible. Assuming that the court decides that this mistake is of the type which would ordinarily justify recission, the court can sever the contract into two "contracts," and order recission of the contract relating to Rose the Second. If the court adopts this approach, Seller is entitled to the return of Rose the Second, and Buyer is entitled to return of $90 which is the portion of purchase price allocated that "separate contract."

EXAMPLE 2. In an early Pennsylvania case, the parties contracted for the sale of timber on a certain tract of land which both parties believed to be owned by vendor. Subsequently, the parties discovered that they were mistaken as to the location of one of vendor's boundaries and that one-third of the contracted-for timber was in fact standing on a tract of land owned by a third party. The court was of the opinion that this mistake was so fundamental that it ordinarily would have justified recission of the agreement. However, prior to the discovery of the mistake, vendee had cut and re-sold some of the timber standing on that portion of the land which was owned by vendor; hence, recission *in toto* was impossible. The court held that under these circumstances, the appropriate remedy was a downward adjustment of the contract price, with restitution to vendee of the amount which represented payment for the timber which was not owned by vendor. This case illustrates that in some situations, restitution will be an appropriate remedy even though recission of the agreement is not possible.

(b) Restitution

When the parties have exchanged anything of value prior to their discovery of the mistake, any order of recission will ordinarily contain, as a concomitant, an order of restitution.

Specific Restitution (Restitution in Specie) of Goods or Land Transferred Pursuant to a Sales Agreement

"Specific restitution" is an equitable decree ordering a return of real or personal property transferred by one or both parties in performance of a contract—usually a contract for the sale of that property. The term is used in contrast to "value restitution" which provides for a money judgment reflecting the value of the property transferred.

When discussing the willingness of the courts to grant specific restitution of property transferred pursuant to a sales contract, one must distinguish between situations where restitution is being sought as a remedy for a *breach* of contract (see § 2.4 (a), supra) and situations in which recission and restitution are being sought as a remedy for *mistake* in the formation of the agreement. As discussed in Chapter Two supra, when relief is sought on the grounds that a purchaser has *breached* a contract for the sale of goods or land, the aggrieved vendor is usually *not* entitled to specific restitution of property which he has already delivered to the purchaser. There are three reasons for the reluctance of the court to grant restitution *in specie* in such cases: (1) When sought as a remedy for breach, the availability of specific restitution is controlled by the requirements for the issuance of equitable decrees generally; thus, specific restitution will not be decreed if a money judgment will be adequate to do justice between the parties. Ordinarily, when a purchaser has defaulted on his obligation to pay for land or goods, a money judgment (i. e. an award of the purchase price) will adequately compensate the aggrieved vendor. (2) When a vendor has transferred land or goods to a purchaser, and the purchaser's only obligation is to pay money in exchange for the land or goods, the purchaser's obligation is considered to be a liquidated debt. Under the "full performance doctrine," (See § 2.4 (a) supra), breach of an obligation to pay a liquidated debt should never provide a basis for restitution (either *in specie* or in value) in favor of the aggrieved vendor. (3) In cases where the vendor has transferred title to *land* to the defaulting purchaser, the courts will not order restitution *in specie* because of the perceived "need for preserving the finality of the deed and the integrity of title to real property." (see § 2.4(a) supra).

In contrast to the above, when relief is sought on the ground of *mistake* in the formation of the contract, the courts consider specific restitution of the property transferred to be a "primary right" of the aggrieved vendor. The "reason" for this is that when such a plaintiff is seeking specific restitution, he is usually doing so as a concomitant to an action for recission. Historically, recission could be obtained only from a court of equity. Once an equity court assumed jurisdiction over an action for recission, it would not then relinquish its jurisdiction merely because a different court (i. e. a law court) could compensate plaintiff through an award of money damages. Thus, most courts and commentators take the position that in cases in which the court has ordered recission on grounds of mistake, there need not be an inquiry as to whether the property is sufficiently unique to justify specific restitution in equity. Instead, an equitable remedy once recognized (i. e. recission) will not be subsequently abandoned merely because of the availability of a different remedy at law by which the vendor can obtain a money judgment for the value of the property.

It must be noted, however, that while the preceding paragraph espouses the position taken by most courts and commentators, the Restatement of Restitution takes a contrary position. Comment d to section 163 of that Restatement provides as follows:

> "Where a transfer of property is avoidable for mistake, and judgment for the return of the property or for its value is not an adequate remedy, the transferor on exercising his power of avoidance can have a decree in a proceeding in equity for the specific restitution of the property. This is the case where land or unique chattels are transferred. *On the other hand, where a judgment at law for the value of the property transferred is an adequate remedy, a court of equity will not decree specific restitution.* (Emphasis supplied)."

EXAMPLE. In *Sherwood v. Walker*, the "pregnant cow" case discussed above, the court found that both parties shared the mutual belief that the cow was barren when, in fact, she was pregnant at the time of sale. This mistaken belief was, according to the court, sufficient to permit recission of the contract. Suppose that prior to the discovery of the mistake, seller had delivered the cow to buyer, and that buyer had paid the purchase price of $80. Suppose further that the market value of a fertile cow was $800. After discovering the mistake, seller brings an action for recission of the

[*254*]

agreement and specific restitution of the cow. Buyer argues that Rose is not a unique cow, and that a judgment at law for the value of Rose ($800 minus the $80 already paid) will be an adequate remedy for seller. According to the view adopted by most courts and commentators, specific restitution should be granted. Because seller's request for restitution *in specie* is merely ancillary to his action for recission, there need not be an inquiry as to whether Rose is a sufficiently unique cow to justify specific restitution in equity. Once the court recognizes the propriety of the main equitable remedy being sought (recission of the contract), that equitable remedy should not then be partially abandoned merely because of the availability of a different remedy at law. However, a contrary result would be reached under section 163 of the Restatement of Restitution. Applying that section, because a judgment at law for the value of the cow ($800 minus the $80 already paid) is an adequate remedy, a court of equity should not grant specific restitution.

Value Restitution (Restitution in Money)

Cases will arise in which the parties have exchanged something of value prior to their discovery of the mistake, yet specific restitution of the benefit exchanged is simply not possible. For example, if the benefit exchanged was in the form of services, obviously those services cannot be returned *in specie.* Another frequently occurring example involves the delivery of goods which the buyer consumes or re-sells prior to discovery of the mistake. In both of these examples, restitution must take the form of the money value of the benefit received.

Services Rendered—Problems of Valuation

When one party has conferred services on another prior to the discovery of the mistake, an order of recission will ordinarily impose an obligation on the recipient to make restitution of the value of those services. In such cases, "value" is usually measured by the amount that such services are worth in the labor market. Sometimes, however, the market value of the services rendered will exceed the value of the actual benefits produced by such services. In such cases, the party conferring the benefits will maintain that the market value of the services themselves (without inquiry into the benefit produced by those services) should be the measure of restitution. The recipient of the services, on the other hand, will argue that he should be liable only to the extent that the services produced something of benefit to him. The resolution of this controversy will usually turn on whether the services rendered were at least part of the thing contracted for. If they are, then the *value of the services themselves* will be the measure of recovery (See EXAMPLE 1, below). If, on the other hand, the services were not part of the bargained-for exchange, and were not requested by the recipient, then restitution is measured by the objective amount by which the recipient benefitted from the conferring of those services. (See EX-AMPLE 2, below).

EXAMPLE 1. Landowner and contractor enter into a contract for the construction of an aesthetically unappealing structure, the existence of which will add nothing to the value of the land. Due to the fraudulent statements of an architect, landowner believes that he is to pay $10,000 for the structure but contractor believes that he is to receive $20,000. After the structure is erected, but before landowner pays for it, the mistake is discovered. Contractor brings an action for recission and restitution. Landowner argues that because the existence of the structure adds nothing to the market value of the land, there should be no monetary recovery. This argument will fail. The mere fact that the landowner bargained for the structure indicates that it has value to him. Because the erection of the structure was the very thing contracted for, contractor is entitled to restitution, measured by the reasonable value of his services. In measuring the value of those services, however, several commentators and the Restatement of Restitution take the position that the two figures believed by the parties to be the contract price should serve as the floor and ceiling on the amount of recovery. Thus, under the facts of this example, contractor would be allowed to recover at least $10,000 but no more than $20,000. Even if the value of the labor and materials was less than $10,000, contractor would be entitled to restitution of $10,000, since that is what Landowner believed the services were worth to him. Similarly, even if the cost of labor and materials exceeds $20,000, contractor's recovery should be limited by that amount since that is what he expected to receive for them.

EXAMPLE 2. Vendor and vendee enter into a contract for the sale of vendor's land. Before title passes, but based on the mutual belief that a valid contract for sale exists, vendee builds a structure on the land, the existence of which will add $5,000 to the market value of the land. The value of the material and labor used in building the structure is $25,000. After the structure is completely built, the parties discover a mistake in the formation of the underlying land transaction, and vendor seeks recission of the agreement. Vendee argues that if recission is granted, she should receive restitution of $25,000, the reasonable value of services rendered prior to discovery of the mistake. Vendee will not be awarded restitution of that amount. Vendor neither bargained for nor requested the construction of the structure and had no intention of keeping the land when the structure was built. He should be liable, therefore, only for the amount

[*258*]

by which he objectively benefitted from the rendering of the services, or $5,000. Suppose however, that Vendor argues that the benefit which he received is zero or less than zero, as he believes that the structure is ugly and will probably tear it down. This argument will not be successful. The measure of restitution (in cases where the services are not bargained for or requested) is the objective (or market) value of the benefits conferred, to the person receiving those benefits. To hold otherwise would be to permit vendor to use the recission to add $5,000 to his net wealth instead of using that remedy to return him to the status quo ante. Moreover, measuring restitution by the objective (market) value of the benefits conferred represents a fair compromise. It avoids the extremes of either measuring restitution by the value of the *services* (which would force vendor to pay for unwanted and possibly nonvaluable services) or, alternatively, measuring restitution by the *subjective value* of the benefits received (which would require an inquiry into vendor's state of mind and might permit him to exploit the mistake for his own economic gain).

Transfer of Goods—Problems of Valuation

When, prior to the discovery of the mistake, one party has transferred goods to another who has then either consumed or otherwise disposed of them, the transferor is ordinarily entitled to restitution based on value of the goods. Ordinarily, ascertaining that value will pose no particular difficulties; the value will simply be the market price of the goods. Because the transferee's alternative source for the goods will usually be the general market, the market price of the goods will be identical to their objective value to the transferee.

Suppose, however, that the transferee has cheaper-than-market source for the goods and that he has accepted the goods under the mistaken belief that they had been sent to him by his cheaper-than-market source. In such a case, the value of the goods to the transferee is less than the market price, and transferor's restitutionary recovery will be limited to this lesser amount.

EXAMPLE. The state has a contract with B under which the state can purchase a certain grade of coal for $3.50 per ton even though the market price for that coal is $4.50 per ton. A, mistakenly believing that she has a contract to furnish coal to the state, delivers 100 tons of coal to the state penitentiary. The penitentiary management, reasonably believing that the coal has been sent to it by B, uses the coal. Upon discovering the mistake, A sues for restitution, arguing that the value of the coal is the market value or $4.50. Because the state could have purchased the coal from B for $3.50 per ton, (and, in fact, believed that it was purchasing from B for $3.50), this latter amount represents the actual value of the benefit to the state. A's restitutionary recovery will be limited to $3.50 per ton.

(c) Recovery of Reliance Losses

When a contract is rescinded on the grounds of mistake in formation, one party may argue that he is entitled to compensation for reliance expenditures which he incurred prior to the discovery of the mistake. The claim for recovery of reliance expenditures will arise in one of two procedural contexts: (1) The plaintiff may be seeking restitution for a benefit which he has transferred to defendant and defendant may be requesting that his reliance expenditures be deducted from plaintiff's restitutionary recovery; or (2) In a case in which there has been no transfer of benefits under the contract, one party may request an affirmative judgment compensating him for reliance losses.

Deduction of Defendant's Reliance Expenditures from Plaintiff's Claim for Restitution

Once it has been decided that a mistake justifies recission of an agreement, it generally follows that neither party is responsible for the other's reliance losses. The reason for this rule is that there is no rational basis for allocating losses between equally innocent parties; therefore, the court should simply leave the losses wherever they happened to lie at the time the mistake was discovered. While, at first blush, this rule may seem equitable, its application can result in hardship. Suppose, for example, that prior to the discovery of the mistake, one party, A, has transferred something of value to the other party, B, and that B has made large expenditures which have not gone into A's pocket. If the contract is subsequently rescinded on the grounds of mistake, A will be entitled to restitution of the benefits which he has conferred on B, but B will not be entitled to a deduction for his reliance expenses because they did not result in any benefit to A. Some commentators have suggested that such a result is unfair and that a contrary result would be more consistent with the rationale which justifies A's claim for restitutionary recovery. That is, when a court allows A's claim for restitution of the benefits which he has conferred on B, it does so on the theory that to allow B to retain those benefits would *unjustly enrich* B at A's expense. But, it is argued, there is nothing *unjust* (or even "enriching") about allowing B to retain that portion of the benefits which is equal to or less than the out-of-pocket expenses which he incurred in reliance on his belief that a valid contract existed. The following example is drawn from a case involving "impossibility" rather than mistake. However, the court's position, as well as the commentators' criticism and proposed solution, is equally applicable to contracts which are rescinded on grounds of mistake.

EXAMPLE. THE FIBROSA CASE, 1942, [1943] A.C. 32. (The full name of this case, which was decided by the House of Lords, is *Fibrosa Spolka Akcyjna v. Fairbairn Lawson Combe Barbour, Limited*). In the summer of 1939 Fairbairn, an English manufacturer of textile machinery, entered a contract with Fibrosa, a Polish textile manufacturer, whereby Fairbairn was to construct in England certain specially designed flax-hackling machines and was then to deliver and install the machines in Poland. Fibrosa paid £ 1000 down on a total purchase price of £ 4800. On September 7, 1939, after Germany had invaded Poland and Germany and England were at war, Fibrosa wrote to Fairbairn stating that since it was evident that the machines could not now be delivered to Poland, Fairbairn should return the down payment of £ 1000. Fairbairn refused to do this, stating that "considerable work has been done upon these machines and we cannot consent to the return of this payment." After further correspondence, Fibrosa brought suit against Fairbairn demanding, among other things, restitution of the down payment. Counsel for Fairbairn argued that it would be unfair to require a return of the £ 1000 paid down, since Fairbairn had expended money on the machines before war broke out and ought to be reimbursed for this reliance expenditure. The court conceded that "No doubt . . . the recipient of the payment may be exposed to hardship if he has to return the money though before the frustration he has incurred the bulk of the expense, and is then left with things on his hands which become valueless to him when the contract fails, so that he gets nothing and has to return the prepayment." However, concluded the court, there was no common-law principle which would permit any apportionment of losses. Thus, to keep within the spirit of the English law the court had either to refuse restitution entirely or to order a return of the whole down payment. The court chose the latter alternative.

While the issue of apportionment of losses has seldom been litigated in the American courts, there are cases which contain dicta indicating that the *Fibrosa* approach will be followed in this country. Most commentators, however, argue that a deduction of part or all defendant's reliance losses from plaintiffs restitution claim would be the more equitable course. A deduction of the reliance expenses could be based on one of two theories: (1) Because the contract (in a case such as *Fibrosa*) called for the manufacture of specific machinery, the defendant, during the period of manufacture, was engaged in the performance of the contract; hence, a benefit (albeit intangible) was conferred on plaintiff as the manufacture progressed. (2) Even in cases in which defendant's expenses were not incurred in the actual performance of the contract (but were, instead, incurred in preparation for performance), equity nevertheless demands an apportionment of the losses.

EXAMPLE. Suppose that the plaintiff in *Fibrosa*, supra, had made a down-payment of 1000 pounds and that defendant had expended 800 pounds on a piece of equipment necessary for the construction of the machinery specified in the contract. Suppose, further, that this equipment could not be used for any other purpose. Defendant's purchase of the equipment would probably be deemed "preparation for performance" rather than actual part performance of the contract. Nevertheless, defendant has purchased the machinery in reliance on his belief that a valid contract was in existence. It seems unfair to force him to return plaintiff's entire down payment (1,000 pounds) given the fact that defendant has expended 800 pounds and has obtained nothing except a piece of equipment which is now worthless to him. If defendant is required to make restitution of the entire 1000 pounds, defendant's net loss will be 800 pounds and plaintiff's net loss will be zero. Those commentators who argue for equitable apportionment of losses maintain that defendant should be permitted a partial deduction for his reliance expenses. In the instant hypothetical, if defendant is permitted a 400 pound deduction, then the losses will be shared equally. Plaintiff will be entitled to restitution of 600 pounds and will thus suffer a net loss of 400 pounds. Defendant, who retains the 400 pounds as partial compensation for an 800 pound reliance expense, will also suffer a net loss of 400 pounds. It must be stressed, however, that this "share-the-losses" approach has not found its way into any known, published American judicial opinions.

Affirmative Judgment Compensating for Reliance Losses

Compensation for reliance losses is sometimes sought by a party even though he has received no benefit from which to deduct such compensation. Here, as in the cases discussed above, the usual approach of the courts is to deny compensation and to leave the reliance losses wherever they happened to lie at the time the mistake was discovered. The rationale, once again, is that there is no reasonable basis for allocating losses between two equally innocent parties. It can be argued, however, that the previously-advanced arguments in favor of apportionment of losses should apply even in those cases where the party who has suffered the losses is seeking compensation by way of affirmative judgment rather than as a deduction from benefits received.

EXAMPLE. In the *Fibrosa* case, supra, if Fairbairn (the party who had spent 800 pounds constructing the machinery) had received no downpayment from Fibrosa, the aforementioned arguments in favor of requiring Fibrosa to share Fairbairn's reliance losses would still apply. That is, if Fibrosa is not required to share Fairbairn's reliance losses, Fairbairn's net loss will be 800 pounds and Fibrosa's net loss will be zero. Since both parties are equally innocent, the losses should be shared. This can be accomplished by granting Fairbairn an affirmative judgment against Fibrosa for 400 pounds.

Moreover, in some situations the parties are not equally innocent. In such cases, the truly innocent party is sometimes awarded compensation for *all* (rather than a portion of) his reliance expenditures on the ground that the other party bore the sole or primary responsibility for causing the mistake.

EXAMPLE. In a post-World War II case, the Australian government invited bids on a sunken oil tanker described as lying on a certain reef "approximately 100 miles north of port X." The plaintiff entered into a contract with the government, paid the contract price of 285 pounds, and began salvage operations. An extensive search was made, but no tanker was located. It was subsequently discovered that the submerged tanker had never existed. In the litigation that followed, the Australian government offered to return the contract price of 285 pounds, but plaintiff argued that this was inadequate since he had spent over 3,000 pounds searching for the nonexistent vessel. In the plaintiff's suit to recover his reliance expenses, the government argued that because this was a case of mutual mistake in the formation of the contract (i. e. the subject matter of contract was never in existence), the court should leave the reliance losses where they happened to lie at the time the mistake was discovered. The court rejected this contention and held the government liable for plaintiff's out-of-pocket expenses. In so holding, the court emphasized that the government had initiated the contract on the basis of very scant evidence that the described tanker actually existed. Thus, while the mistake could technically be described as a mutual mistake of existing material fact, it was, in fact, caused by the negligence of the government. This was not a case which required the court to apportion losses between two equally innocent parties. Instead, it was a case where one party was primarily culpable; thus, it was deemed equitable to condition recission not only on restitution of the contract price of 285 pounds but also on payment of plaintiff's reliance expenses of 3000 pounds.

CHAPTER 12

MISTAKE IN INTEGRATION OR EXPRESSION—THE REFORMATION REMEDY

§ 12.1 General Principles

A mistake in "integration" occurs whenever the parties have reached an agreement which they intend to express in writing, but because of an error, the writing does not correctly express the agreement. The appropriate remedy for this type of mistake is reformation, a process by which the court "re-writes" the written instrument to make it conform to the true agreement of the parties. Courts, in granting reformation, have repeatedly stressed that the purpose of the remedy is not to make new contract for the parties but instead to enforce the contract that they have made for themselves. Thus, reformation is granted only when three elements coalesce: (1) An agreement between the parties, (2) A writing which was intended to embody that agreement, and (3) A discrepancy between the agreement and the writing. In such cases, the writing is simply "reformed" to conform to the agreement. (See Example 1 infra). It follows as a corollary that when the writing is not at variance with the parties' underlying agreement, there should be no reformation. (See Example 2 infra).

EXAMPLE 1. Vendor and vendee enter into an oral agreement for the conveyance of a certain parcel of land. The parties have both examined the land, and both know its exact location, description and boundaries. Because of an error in drafting, the deed, when executed and delivered, describes 1000 square feet more land than was agreed upon. This extra land is not owned by vendor and is not part of the property bargained for. Upon application of the vendor, and after production of satisfactory evidence as to the terms of the underlying agreement of the parties, the court will reform the deed so that it embodies the actual agreement.

EXAMPLE 2. City X invites and receives bids on the construction of a proposed building. Contractor Y bids $240,000. A few days after his bid is accepted by the City, Y discovers that he made an error in computation and that his bid should have been $250,000 instead of $240,000. Ordinarily, Y will be entitled to no relief. But, if the disparity between Y's bid and all the other bids is sufficient to charge the City with notice of the error, then Y may be permitted to *rescind* the agreement. (See § 11.1(d) supra). However, it is difficult to conceive of a set of circumstances which would justify *reformation* of the contract price to $250,000. There is no discrepancy between the writing and the underlying agreement because the parties have never agreed to the $250,000 price.

Thus, if the court were to allow reformation it would be making a new contract for the parties rather than merely enforcing a contract which they made for themselves.

§ 12.2   Difference Between Reformation and Recission

The remedy of reformation is the diametrical opposite of the remedy of recission. Because recission puts an end to an agreement, it often serves to thwart the intention of at least one of the parties. Reformation, on the other hand, upholds the transaction and serves to give effect to the intentions of both parties. Because reformation is a contract-sustaining rather than a contract-negating remedy, many of the rules relating to reformation are different from the rules relating to recission. Three of these differences are discussed below.

(a) Size or Gravity of Mistake

When *recission* is sought as a remedy for mistake, it is often said that the mistake must be "material" or "basic." The underlying rationale is that it is usually the aim of the law to enforce rather than negate a contract. Thus, it is only a very grave or sizable mistake which will override the general policy supporting the upholding of agreements. *Reformation*, on the other hand, upholds and enforces the contract. Thus, it should be irrelevant whether the mistake is large or small.

In either case, reformation, which simply eliminates the mistake, will bring about the contract which the parties actually intended. It must be noted, however, that the Restatement of Contracts takes a contrary position and will not allow reformation unless there is a "material" variance between the agreement of the parties and its written expression. It is the position of several commentators that the Restatement position is erroneous and that the error probably stems from a failure to differentiate between the remedies of recission and reformation.

(b) Mutuality of Mistake

As has been previously discussed, *recission* of a contract will ordinarily not be granted unless the mistake is mutual. The policy underlying this rule is that the purpose of contract law is to fulfill the reasonable expectations of the parties to a bargain. The reasonable expectations of one party should not be set aside merely because the other party was in error. In contrast, reformation, when properly granted, never entails the setting aside of the reasonable expectations of either party. Thus, one would assume that in reformation cases, the "mutuality" of the mistake would be irrelevant. While that is the position taken by most commentators, several courts have espoused a contrary position, holding that only a "mutual" mistake of the parties will permit reformation. That such a rule can lead to unjust results can be seen from the following example.

EXAMPLE. Vendor and vendee enter into an oral agreement for the conveyance of a certain parcel of land. The parties have both examined the land, and both know its exact location, description and boundaries. Because of an error in drafting, the deed, when executed and delivered, describes 1000 square feet more land than was agreed upon. When vendee receives the deed, he immediately realizes that the extra 1000 feet is not part of the property bargained for. He nevertheless accepts the deed, hoping to capitalize on vendor's mistake. When vendor discovers the mistake, he brings an action to have the deed reformed. Vendee defends on the ground that he was aware of the mistake; hence it was not mutual. If the court applies the "rule" that only a "mutual" mistake will permit reformation, the anamolous result will be that a totally innocent vendee would be required to submit to a reformation of the instrument, but a vendee who acts fraudulently or at least knowingly will be allowed to take advantage of the other party's error. Realizing the absurdity of this result, courts will often grant reformation in this type of case on the ground that there was a mistake on one side and fraud or inequitable conduct on the other. But, this "mistake plus inequity" rationale serves only to complicate the analysis. Several commentators have maintained that it would be better simply to recognize that when reformation is sought, the mutuality of the mistake is irrelevant. Instead, the focus ought to be on the *mutuality in the underlying agreement*; for if there is mutuality in the underlying agreement, then there can be no reasonable expectations based on a written instrument which is not in conformity with that agreement. This is true regardless of whether or not the mistake was "mutual" and regardless of whether or not one of the parties acted fraudulently or inequitably. Thus, in the instant example, if both parties agreed to the exchange of a parcel of land containing X feet, then there can be no reasonable expectation that the vendee is entitled to X plus 1,000 feet, and this is true regardless of whether the mistake was mutual and regardless of whether the vendee acted fraudulently or inequitably.

(c) Negligence Not a Bar to Reformation

Because reformation, when properly granted, will always entail an upholding of the reasonable expectations of the parties, negligence on the part of plaintiff (usually consisting of a failure to read the writing) should not serve as a bar to a court's willingness to reform an instrument. While there are occasional statements to the effect that negligence is a bar to reformation, those statements inevitably appear in cases where the elements necessary for reformation do not exist, and hence reformation would have been denied even in the absence of plaintiff's negligence.

EXAMPLE. Tenant and landlord entered into an oral lease agreement. According to tenant's allegations, the agreement contained certain provisions favorable to tenant, relating to taxes and insurance. The subsequently-executed written lease was silent as to taxes and insurance, and tenant sought to have the lease reformed so as to include those terms. In denying reformation the court indicated that tenant should have read the lease prior to signing it and that his failure to do so constituted negligence which would bar reformation. The court then concluded its opinion with a review of the evidence and held that tenant had failed to furnish "satisfactory proof" that landlord had actually agreed to the terms relating to insurance and taxes. The court's holding rendered unnecessary its discussion of plaintiff's negligence in failing to read the written lease. Because plaintiff had failed to prove mutuality of agreement regarding the tax and insurance provisions, it follows that plaintiff also failed to establish a discrepancy between the written instrument and the underlying agreement. Thus, plaintiff has simply failed to prove that there was a mistake in integration, and it was that failure rather than his failure to read the instrument which should have served as the basis for the court's denial of reformation.

§ 12.3 Mistake as to Legal Effect of Words Used

In the previously-discussed situations involving mistakes in integration, the mistake consisted of using words different from those which the parties intended to use. In some early cases, it was sometimes stated that reformation should be limited to mistakes of that type and that reformation should be denied when the parties have used the very words which they intended to use but were mistaken about the legal effect of those words. There did not, however, seem to be any rational basis for denying reformation in such cases because they, too, resulted in a written instrument which was at variance with the underlying agreement of the parties. Thus, in recent years, the courts have departed from the position that reformation should be denied automatically when the mistake is merely one of "legal effect" and have, instead, shown a willingness to grant reformation for any discrepancy between a written instrument and an underlying agreement regardless of whether that mistake consists of the use of unintended words or of use of intended words, the legal effect of which was misunderstood.

EXAMPLE. A, B, and C enter into a business venture in which they agree that if a certain condition occurs, B and C will be jointly liable to A. It is the parties' understanding that the term "joint liability" encompasses both joint liability and individual liability on the part of B and C. Because of their mistake as to the legal effect of the words they have chosen, their written agreement provides only for "joint liability" rather than for "joint and several liability," even though this latter term would have correctly expressed their actual agreement. When A becomes aware of the mistake, she sues for reformation of the agreement. Under the older view, reformation would have been denied because the parties used the very words which they had agreed upon; their mistake was simply that they did not understand the legal meaning of those words. Under the more modern view, reformation will be granted since reformation will serve to sustain the agreement which the parties actually intended, as opposed to the "agreement" which is embodied in the writing.

§ 12.4 Reformation and the Parol Evidence Rule

The parol evidence rule (a subject which is generally beyond the scope of this text) provides that terms which are set forth in a writing which the parties *intend* to be a "final integration" (i. e. a complete and final expression of the agreement) may not be contradicted by evidence of prior oral or written agreements or of contemporaneous oral agreements. If one focuses on the word "intend," it seems clear that the parol evidence rule can never be an obstacle to reformation as a remedy for mistake in integration. That is, the parol evi-

dence rule bars evidence of prior agreements only
if the written instrument was *intended* to be a
complete and final statement of the agreement.
If one party is alleging a mistake in integration,
the essence of that allegation is that the writing
was *not* what the parties *intended* as their agreement, i. e. it was not intended to be a "final
integration."   As Professor Corbin has stated:
"The parol evidence rule does not itself purport to
establish the fact of 'integration'; and until that
fact is established, the 'rule' does not purport to
have any legal operation."   Therefore, the rule
would not bar the party seeking reformation from
introducing evidence of the prior oral agreement
for purposes of showing that the written instrument was not intended to be an integration of that
agreement.   And, if the trier of fact finds that the
parties did make the oral agreement and intended
its terms to be effective, then that oral agreement
is effective even though it contradicts the terms of
the written instrument; for, a finding that the
oral agreement was intended to be the effective
agreement is also a finding that the inconsistent
writing was not intended to be a final integration
of the agreement.

§ 12.5 Reformation and the Statute of Frauds

(a) Executory Contracts

While the courts and commentators have been
almost unanimous in stating that the parol evi-

dence rule is not an obstacle to reforming a contract, there is considerable difference of opinion over the effect of the Statute of Frauds as a bar to reformation of an executory written agreement. Suppose, for example, that vendor and vendee enter into an oral agreement for the sale of Blackacre and Whiteacre. The parties subsequently reduce their agreement to writing, but due to an error in drafting, the writing omits Whiteacre. Vendee seeks to have the written instrument reformed. Vendor defends on the ground that reformation would be tantamount to enforcing an oral contract to convey Whiteacre and that the remedy should therefore be denied on the grounds that it would violate the Statute of Frauds.

There appear to be at least three views concerning the availability of reformation in the above example. First, there is the position of the Restatement of Contracts that no executory written contract can be reformed if reformation would require the inclusion of an oral promise which, under the Statute of Frauds, is required to be in writing. The reason given to support this position is that the incorporation of the oral promise into the writing renders the oral promise enforceable. The result is that an unenforceable oral contract (in the instant case, an agreement to convey Whiteacre) is enforced. "The Statute bars enforcement of an executory oral promise within its scope not less when an *incorrect* writing is made than when *no* writing is made." Restatement of Contracts § 509, Comment A [emphasis supplied].

The second view, espoused by Professor Palmer and by many courts, is that reformation is a correction of a written contract, not enforcement of an oral contract. Palmer argues that the Restatement position "discounts as of no significance a fact that most courts have found *is* significant, that is, the attempt of the parties, frustrated through error, to put their agreement in a form that would make it legally effective under the Statute." Thus, the existence of the writing should satisfy the policy of the Statute of Frauds even though it is not the terms of that writing which are being enforced, and, even though the court must turn to the oral agreement in order to ascertain the correct terms of the contract.

While Palmer's view seems technically correct —that is, correction of a written contract is not the same thing as "enforcement" of the underlying oral agreement, his view fails to recognize the fact that the party seeking reformation is doing so for the purpose of providing a basis for enforcement of the oral promise either in the same or a subsequent lawsuit. If the Statute of Frauds is premised on a distrust of evidence of certain types of oral agreements, then it seems (to this writer) that the policy of the Statute is violated any time that enforceability will, at any stage of the proceedings, depend on proof that such an oral agreement was made. Thus, it appears that the Restatement is correct in regarding as insignificant the *attempt* of the parties to put their oral agreement in a form that would make it enforceable under the statute. Indeed, if Professor Palmer's approach is carried to its logical conclusion, then *any* attempt of the parties to put the agreement into written form would satisfy the Statute of Frauds. For example, if the parties had signed a written document which was subsequently lost or destroyed, then the courts would have to permit proof of the oral agreement in a suit for *direct* enforcement of that agreement, for there would be no written document which could be reformed. Assuming the courts would not permit such a flagrant direct violation of the Statute of Frauds, it follows that they probably should not permit reformation to be used as a vehicle for indirect circumvention of the Statute. On the other hand, given the prevailing judicial antipathy towards the Statute, perhaps any type of indirect circumvention will find favor with the courts.

The third view concerning the effect of the Statute of Frauds as a bar to reformation is that reformation may be granted as a means to prevent unjust enrichment but not to enforce the expectation interest. Thus, in the example under discussion, the oral agreement was for the sale and purchase of Blackacre and Whiteacre, but the writing omitted Whiteacre. Reformation in such a case should be denied because the ultimate effect of this remedy would be to give the vendee his expectancy under an unenforceable contract (i. e. the right to the conveyance of Whiteacre), a result which would violate the policy of the Statute. If, on the other hand, the oral agreement was to sell Blackacre only, but the written instrument mistakenly provided for the sale of both Blackacre and Whiteacre, a reformation of the contract which results in the deletion of Whiteacre would not result in giving either party his expectancy under an unenforceable contract. Instead, each party would obtain his expectancy under an *enforceable* term of the contract because the promise relating to the sale of Blackacre is already embodied in the unreformed writing. In such a case, reformation would simply prevent unjust enrichment by preventing vendee from obtaining two tracts of land when he has only bargained for one.

Statute of Frauds No Bar to Defensive Plea of Mistake in Integration

If a court adopts either the first or third view espoused above, and holds that a writing cannot be reformed when the result will be the enforcement of an unenforceable agreement, it does not follow that the mistaken written contract itself will be enforced. Instead, the mistake in integration can be used as a defense to enforcement of the written agreement. Thus, in the example under discussion if the oral contract is for Blackacre and Whiteacre, and the writing incorrectly omits Whiteacre, even if the court holds that vendee cannot have the contract reformed, it does not follow that vendor can enforce the provision relating to Blackacre. If he attempts to do so, vendee can assert the mistake defensively and thereby obtain recission of the executory agreement.

(b) Executed Contracts

Once a contract has been executed, the Statute of Frauds is generally not an obstacle to reformation.

EXAMPLE. Vendor and vendee enter into an oral contract for the sale of Blackacre and Whiteacre. The parties subsequently execute the agreement by delivery of the deed and payment of the purchase price for both parcels of land. It is then discovered that, due to a mistake, the deed does not include Whiteacre. In most jurisdictions, vendee will be entitled to reformation. However, in at least one jurisdiction, Massachusetts, reformation will be refused on the grounds that it would add to the land conveyed and thus would be tantamount to enforcement of an oral agreement to convey Whiteacre. The majority view appears to be the better one. Once a land contract has actually been executed, most courts will be reluctant to *rescind* the transaction. Here, the deed to Blackacre has already been conveyed, and most courts will wish to respect the "finality" of that transaction. Hence, if the deed is not reformed so as to include a conveyance of Whiteacre, vendor will be unjustly enriched in that he will have conveyed only one parcel of land but will have received payment for two.

CHAPTER 13

MISTAKE IN PERFORMANCE OF AN OBLIGATION—THE RESTITUTION REMEDY

§ 13.1 General Principles

A mistake in performance occurs whenever one party confers a benefit (usually money) on the other party that is not called for by the contract. In such cases, the party conferring the benefit is entitled to restitution on the grounds that retention of the benefit will unjustly enrich the party retaining it.

EXAMPLE. Under a contract between S and B for the sale of widgets for $1,000, B pays $200 in advance of delivery. After receiving the widgets, B, who has forgotten about the partial pre-payment, pays the entire purchase price of $1,000. S, who may or may not have forgotten about the pre-payment, deposits the $1,000 in her bank account. Upon discovery of the mistake, B seeks restitution of the $200 overpayment. The remedy will be granted; S's retention of the $200 would be unjust enrichment in the clearest sense of the phrase. Because of B's mistake, S has received a money payment to which she is not entitled and her only claim for retention of the $200 is that she is now in possession of it.

The salient feature of "mistake in performance" cases is that the court can grant the requested relief without rescinding the contract or any portion of it. The court is required to set aside only the overpayment or other benefit, but not part of the underlying transaction. Thus, the "mistake in performance" cases share an important feature in common with "mistake in integration" cases; in both, the court is *upholding* (rather than negating) the underlying agreement and formulating a remedy which ensures that the actions of the parties are in conformity with that agreement. The consequences of this shared feature are that in the "mistake in performance" cases, as in "mistake in integration" cases, neither the size of the mistake, nor its unilateral nature, nor the plaintiff's negligence should present an obstacle to recovery. (See § 12.2(a), (b) and (c) supra). Thus, in the preceding example, it is immaterial that the overpayment was "only" $200, that defendant may have been aware of the error, and that it clearly was a result of plaintiff's negligence. Unlike the "mistake in formation" cases, the defendant who benefits from a mistake in performance has no contractual expectation interest in the extra sum which she has received. Her receipt of the benefit is simply a windfall, and she is in no position to argue (as can a defendant in some "mistake in formation" cases) that the relief sought will deprive her of the benefit of a bargain. Since there are no equities in defendant's favor, and the court is not being asked to set aside a contract, the size, unilaterality, and responsibility for the mistake should all be irrelevant.

§ 13.2   Denial of Restitution When Retention of the Benefit Is Not Unjust

In the usual case of mistake in performance, the basis for plaintiff's claim is that defendant has no right or entitlement to the benefit which he has received, and that retention of that benefit would unjustly enrich the defendant at plaintiff's expense. Because the presence of unjust enrichment is the sine qua non of plaintiff's claim, it follows that when defendant's retention of the benefit is not deemed unjust or inequitable, restitution will be denied. In such cases, plaintiff will not be entitled to relief even though he conferred the benefit in the mistaken belief that he was under a legal obligation to do so. There are three typical "mistake in performance" situations in which the absence of unjust enrichment leads to a denial of restitution: (1) Cases in which plaintiff, while not under a legal obligation to pay defendant, is under a moral obligation to do so; [See EXAMPLE 1 below]; (2) Cases in which defendant is not the person to whom plaintiff owed the particular obligation at issue, but defendant does have a different claim against plaintiff and is retaining this benefit in satisfaction [See EXAMPLE 2 below]; and (3) Cases in which plaintiff has made a mistake in performing a contract with the defendant but the over-performance results in a benefit to a third person rather than to defendant. [See EXAMPLE 3 below].

EXAMPLE 1.   Plaintiff borrows $5,000 from defendant, and gives defendant a promissory note for that amount.   Eight years later, not realizing that the debt is barred by the statute of limitations, plaintiff pays back the $5,000 plus interest.   After learning that he was under no legal obligation to pay, plaintiff seeks restitution on the grounds of mistake.   Relief will be denied.   Plaintiff was morally, although not legally obligated to re-pay the loan.   Defendant's retention of the "mistaken" repayment is not deemed to be unjust.

EXAMPLE 2.   R, Retailer, buys hoola hoops from Jones Manufacturing Company in Cleveland and ping pong balls from a different Jones Manufacturing Company in New York.   Payment of the purchase price for both the hoola hoops and the ping pong balls is due on June 1.   On June 1, being on the brink of insolvency, R decides to make payment only to the New York Company, as he has a need for further business dealings with that firm.   Due to a clerical error, R's check is sent to the Cleveland firm.   Because the check is accompanied by a note which reads "payment for 1,000 boxes of ping pong balls," the Cleveland firm has reason to know that a mistake has been made. Nevertheless, that company deposits R's check. If R brings a suit for restitution, relief will be denied. Even though there was a mistake in performance (because R did not intend to make payment to the Cleveland firm) retention of the payment is not deemed to be unjust. Because the Cleveland company does have a valid claim against R, it should be permitted to retain the payment in full or partial satisfaction of that claim.

EXAMPLE 3. C, a building contractor, is under contract to remodel two floors of a five-story building. C subcontracts with S for S to paint the interiors of those two floors. By mistake, S paints all five floors of the building. S seeks restitution from C for the reasonable value of the services rendered in painting the three extra floors. Relief will be denied. Because C was merely a contractor with respect to the first two floors, S's over-performance, though made for the purpose of performing a contract with C, resulted in benefits to third persons rather than to C. Since C is retaining no benefits, he is not being unjustly enriched.

§ 13.3 Insurance Contracts: "Mistake in Performance" Distinguished from "Assumption of Risk"

Cases frequently occur in which an insurance company has made a payment on the assumption that the contingency insured against has happened when in fact it has not. There is a split of authority as to whether the insurer is entitled to restitution in such situations. Those courts which allow recovery usually analyze the case as one involving a simple mistake in performance for which restitution should be granted. Those courts which refuse to grant relief usually base their decision on one (or both) of two factors: (1) The need for finality of insurance payments; and (2) The fact that the insurance company has "assumed the risk" of the non-occurrence of the event insured against. This latter analysis is most often found in cases in which the existence of the event was in dispute from the outset and the insurance company has paid only part of the amount due in settlement of the claim.

EXAMPLE 1. Upon disappearance of the insured, beneficiary (who believes that the insured is dead) makes a claim under insured's life insurance policy. Insurer disputes the fact of death and eventually settles the matter by paying one third of the amount due under the policy. When it is later proved that the insured is alive, insurer seeks restitution of the amount paid. Most courts would deny recovery (assuming that beneficiary has not acted fraudulently). Insurer knew that it did not know the true facts and paid anyway, thereby "assuming the risk" that insured was still alive. Moreover, the initial dispute over the validity of the claim coupled with insurer's payment and beneficiary's acceptance of much less than the full amount of the claim is proof that the parties intended the arrangement to be a final settlement

[*290*]

agreement. The implicit terms of this agreement were that beneficiary was relinquishing his claim for the larger amount and insurer was relinquishing his right to deny the validity of the claim. Unlike the ordinary "mistake in performance" case, restitution, here, would require recission of the settlement agreement and would, therefore, violate the expectations of at least one of the parties to that agreement.

EXAMPLE 2. Upon disappearance of the insured, beneficiary (who believes that the insured is dead) makes a claim under insured's life insurance policy. Insurer does not dispute the fact of death and pays the entire amount due under the policy. When it is later proved that the insured is alive, insurer seeks restitution of the amount paid. There is a split of authority as to whether relief should be granted in this situation. Those courts which deny recovery do so on the grounds that insurer should have known of its own ignorance regarding the death of the insured and that the company therefore assumed the risk that the insured was still alive. Thus, this is not a case of mistake but one of conscious ignorance, for which restitution should be denied.

Those courts which allow restitution in cases such as the one under discussion do so on the ground that there will be unjust enrichment of beneficiary if he is allowed to retain a payment made under a life insurance policy when there has, in fact, been no death. Those courts analyze the case as one of simple mistake in performance—the company has made the payment believing that it was under a legal obligation to do so when, in fact, it was not. Some of these opinions further justify recovery on the ground that to refuse restitution will encourage insurers to deny claims when the slightest doubt exists and will force many insureds and beneficiaries into expensive litigation even in cases in which the validity of the claim is not in serious dispute.

CHAPTER 14

UNCONSCIONABILITY

§ 14.1 Historical Background

The concept of "unconscionability," deeply rooted in our system of equity, seems to defy definition. It has generally been defined as that which "affronts the chancellor's sense of decency" and/or "shocks the conscience of the court." The amorphous nature of the concept has always proved troublesome. As one Seventeenth Century legal philosopher stated: "One Chancellor has a long foot, another a short foot, a third an indifferent foot: 'tis the same thing in the Chancellor's conscience."

Despite these longstanding criticisms of the vague and open-ended concept, equity courts frequently did (and still do) find contractual provisions to be "unconscionable." Equity's remedial response to a finding of unconscionability was either a rescinding of the agreement or refusal to grant specific enforcement.

In contrast to the courts of equity, the courts of law rarely relied on unconscionability as a reason for refusing to enforce an agreement. When a contract was deemed oppressive, the law courts would not condemn it as "unconscionable" but would, instead, employ "covert" or "surreptitious" tools to prevent enforcement of the agreement.

[*293*]

By a stretching and distorting of various legal doctrines, the courts would invalidate offending contracts by finding "defects" such as a mistake, ambiguity, and lack of consideration even in cases where it was quite clear that those defects did not really exist.

EXAMPLE. Lender and borrower entered into an agreement under which, in exchange for a $5000 loan, borrower promised to repay the principal and 8% interest and also to pay lender, a bank president, $100 per month for as long as borrower remained in business. Borrower repaid the $5000 together with 8% interest but refused to pay the $100 monthly, arguing that the provision was unconscionable. The court refused to hold the provision unconscionable but invalidated it nevertheless. The court reasoned that the $5000 loan was consideration for the repayment of the principal plus interest but that there was no consideration for borrower's promise to pay the $100 per month. Hence, that "separate promise" was unenforceable.

The law court's use of such "covert tools" in order to produce "justice" in individual cases often produced results which were illogical and of doubtful precedential value. As Karl Llewellyn, the principal draftsman of the Uniform Commercial Code, noted, "Covert tools are never reliable tools." Thus it was the primary purpose of UCC 2-302, the Code provision on unconscionability, to encourage courts to openly acknowledge that they were invalidating contracts on the grounds of oppressiveness rather than continuing to conjure up pretexts in order to achieve the same result.

§ 14.2   The Uniform Commercial Code Provision on Unconscionability, UCC 2–302

UCC 2–302 provides as follows:

(1) If the court as a matter of law finds the contract or any clause of the contract to have been unconscionable at the time it was made, the court may refuse to enforce the contract, or it may enforce the remainder of the contract without the unconscionable clause, or it may so limit the application of any unconscionable clause as to avoid any unconscionable result.

(2) When it is claimed or appears to the court that the contract or any clause thereof may be unconscionable the parties shall be afforded a reasonable opportunity to present evidence as to its commercial setting, purpose and effect to aid the court in making the determination.

The legislative purpose of this provision is explained in the opening language of Official Comment #1:

"This section is intended to make it possible for the courts to police explicitly against the contracts or clauses which they find to be unconscionable. In the past such policing has been accomplished by adverse construction of language, by manipulation of the rules of offer and acceptance or by determinations that the clause is contrary to public policy or to the dominant purpose of the contract. This section is intended to allow the court to pass directly on the unconscionability of the contract or particular clause therein and to make a conclusion of law as to its unconscionability. The basic test is whether, in the light of the general commercial background and the commercial needs of the particular trade or case, the clauses involved are so one-sided as to be unconscionable under the circumstances existing at the time of the making of the contract. Subsection (2) makes it clear that it is proper for the court to hear evidence upon these questions. *The principle is one of the prevention of oppression and unfair surprise* [Citation omitted] *and not of disturbance of allocation of risks because of superior bargaining power."* [emphasis supplied]

The "principle" contained in the comment does not seem particularly helpful. As Professors White and Summers have noted: "It is simply a string of hopelessly subjective synonyms laden with a heavy 'value' burden: 'oppression,' 'unfair,' or 'one-sided.' . . . How a court can refuse to enforce certain contracts which were formerly enforceable and not at the same time disturb the allocation of the risk because of superior bargaining power, is difficult to see."

§ 14.3 The Case Law

Because it is impossible to define "unconscionability" objectively, it seems useful to look at the case law in order to ascertain which types of clauses have actually been invalidated. The most frequently-occurring cases in which the courts have found clauses to be unconscionable can be grouped into three categories: (a) Cases in which there is a lack of "meaningful choice" on the part of one of the parties during the process of contract formation; (b) Cases in which the price of the item(s) sold is deemed to be excessive; and (c) Cases in which one party (usually the seller) expands his own remedial rights and/or unduly limits the remedies available to the other party.

(a) Absence of "Meaningful Choice"

Invalidation of a contract because of the lack of a "meaningful choice" during the "bargaining" process (often termed "procedural unconscionability") usually occurs only after a judicial finding of sharp practices on the part of the seller and/or ignorance on the part of the buyer. In such cases, the contract is deemed unconscionable in that the buyer has made a choice that was less than fully informed.

EXAMPLE. In the landmark case of *Williams v. Walker-Thomas Furniture Co.*, 350 F.2d 445 (D.C.Cir. 1965), the defendant-consumer was a welfare mother with seven children and an income of $218 per month. Over a five-year period, she purchased $1800 of merchandise from plaintiff Walker-Thomas; and, at the time of her default, she had already paid the store $1400. The agreement between Ms. Williams and Walker-Thomas contained a very complicated installment payment provision which the court characterized as "rather obscure." The net effect of that provision was that the store retained a balance due and a security interest in *each* item sold until the entire account (for all items) was paid. When Ms. Williams eventually defaulted, the store sought to replevy all items purchased during the five year period even though her total payments left a balance due of less than the purchase price of the most recently purchased item, a stereo set which cost $515. The trial court granted the judgment of replevin and the first appellate court affirmed; but the Circuit Court of Appeals for the District of Columbia reversed and remanded for findings on the issue of unconscionability. In discussing the standards to be applied, the court stated:

Unconscionability has generally been recognized to include an absence of meaningful choice on the part of one of the parties together with contract terms which are unreasonably favorable to the other party. Whether a meaningful choice is present in a particular case can only be determined by consideration of all the circumstances surrounding the transaction. In many cases the meaningfulness of the choice is negated by a gross inequality of bargaining power. The manner in which the contract was entered is also relevant to this consideration.

The court then indicated that Ms. Williams' lack of education, coupled with the use of fine print and other "deceptive sales practices" by the seller, might vitiate the meaningfulness of Ms. Williams' choice:

Did each party to the contract, considering his obvious education or lack of it, have a reasonable opportunity to understand the terms of the contract, or were the important terms hidden in a maze of fine print and minimized by deceptive sales practices? . . . In such a case the usual rule that the terms of the agreement are not to be questioned should be abandoned and the court should consider whether the terms of the contract are so unfair that enforcement should be withheld.

(b) *Excessive Price*

There appears to be a split of authority as to whether excessiveness of price, in and of itself, is a sufficient basis for finding a contract unconscionable. Moreover, those courts which do consider this factor (either by itself or together with other factors) to be grounds for invalidation, are not in agreement as to the criteria by which "excessiveness" is to be judged. Some focus on the amount of profit made by the seller, others look at what other merchants are charging for similar items, and still others seem to be concerned only with the amount of the seller's mark-up, without regard to profit.

EXAMPLE. In the oft-cited case of *American Home Improvement Inc. v. MacIver*, 105 N.H. 435, 201 A.2d 886 (1964) the parties entered into an agreement for the sale and installation of home siding for a price of $2,568. Buyer defaulted and seller sued for payment. At trial, the evidence indicated that the goods and services had a value of $959 and that the remainder of the price was based on an $800 commission and finance charges of $809. The court held, inter alia, that the contract was unconscionable on account of the excessiveness of the price. In measuring "excessiveness" the court seemed concerned only with the size of seller's mark up and did not even discuss what other merchants charged for similar siding or whether this particular seller had made an "excessive" profit on the transaction.

(c) Contractual Expansion or Limitation of Remedy

In a third group of cases, a contract (or one of its provisions) will be invalidated because one of the parties (usually the seller) has expanded his own remedial rights and/or unduly limited the remedies available to the other party.

When a seller expands his own remedial rights beyond those ordinarily available under the UCC he usually does so by fixing liquidated damages for non-acceptance. Liquidated damages clauses are governed by UCC 2–718. See Chapter 9, supra.

In lieu of (or in addition to) expanding his own remedies, a seller will frequently limit or modify the buyer's remedies. Contractual modifications and/or limitations of remedy are governed by UCC 2–719. Thus, when a buyer is claiming that a contract is unconscionable because of a provision which has unduly restricted his remedies, the case will be governed by UCC 2–719 as well as by UCC 2–302. Contractual limitations on remedies under 2–719 is the subject of Chapter 10, supra. However, 2–719(3)'s incorporation of the "unconscionability" concept will be discussed at this point.

UCC 2–719(3) provides as follows:

> Consequential damages may be limited or excluded unless the limitation or exclusion is unconscionable. Limitation of consequential damages for injury to the person in the case of consumer goods is prima facie unconscionable but limitation of damages where the loss is commercial is not.

According to this subsection, in every case in which a buyer has purchased consumer goods which cause personal injuries, there is a presumption that any clause limiting damages for those personal injuries is unconscionable. Several commentators have stated that, in theory, this is only a presumption and can be overcome by the seller. Theory aside, however, this author has not been able to find any case in which a seller of consumer goods has successfully excluded damages for personal injuries.

In all other situations (i. e. transactions in which the buyer is not a consumer as well as cases in which a consumer-buyer has suffered injury other than "injury to the person"), the buyer has the burden of proving the unconscionability of the clause which excludes or limits consequential damages. In determining whether buyer has met this burden, the courts will look primarily at two factors: (1) Whether the contractual limitation has left the buyer with "at least a fair quantum of remedy for breach" [UCC 2–719, Official Comment #1]; and (2) Whether the buyer was able to make a "meaningful choice" during the "bargaining" process.

EXAMPLE. Buyer purchases a sailboat from seller. In large and conspicuous language, the contract limits buyer's remedies to repair or replacement of defective parts, or, when necessary, replacement of the entire boat. The agreement specifically states (again in conspicuous language) that seller is not liable for any consequential damages, including those arising from both personal injuries and injury to property. Seller explains both of these clauses to buyer and also explains that the rudders on some of seller's boats have been malfunctioning. Due to a defect, the rudder on the boat purchased by buyer malfunctions while he is sailing it. The sailboat collides with a large yacht. As a result, the sailboat is totally destroyed and causes damage to the yacht. Buyer's child, a passenger in the boat, is seriously injured. Seller willingly replaces the sailboat (with a non-defective one) but argues that he has effectively excluded liability for consequential damages. Buyer will be able to recover for his child's injuries. There is probably nothing that seller can do to overcome the presumption of unconscionability regarding that part of the clause which excludes liability for personal injuries. On the other hand, the clause is *not* prima facie unconscionable in so far as it excludes consequential damages for damage to the yacht. Moreover, buyer will probably not be able to prove that the exclusion of damages arising from injury to the yacht is unconscionable *in fact*. Buyer has been left with "a fair quantum of remedy for breach" (seller, pursuant to the replacement clause, furnished buyer with a new boat). Moreover, assuming that buyer is a person of average intelligence, it will be difficult to prove that he was not able to make a meaningful choice during the bargaining process. The clauses limiting liability not only were in conspicuous language but also were explained to him. He was aware of the fact that the rudder was possibly defective and should have known that such a defect could result in damage to other property. Hence, the limitation on consequential damage, in so far as it relates to damage to the yacht, is conscionable and will probably be upheld.

Transactions in Which Both Parties Are Businessmen

When both parties to a transaction are businessmen, the courts are usually reluctant to strike remedial limitations as unconscionable. An experienced businessman will usually find it difficult to prove that he was unable to make a meaningful choice during the bargaining process. In the words of one appellate judge, such buyers are "hardly the sheep keeping company with wolves. . . ." Likewise, many courts, referring to the language of 2–719, Official Comment #3, note that as between businessmen, limitations on consequential damages "are merely an allocation of unknown or undeterminable risk" and should not be disturbed by the judiciary.

But, not all businessmen are equally "experienced;" and there are a few cases, involving poorly educated merchants, in which courts have invalidated remedial limitations on grounds akin to absence of meaningful choice in the bargaining process.

EXAMPLE. A contract between an oil company and a gas station operator excluded consequential damages resulting from the Company's failure to make timely deliveries. The Company made several late deliveries, causing the operator to lose substantial profits. The court noted that the buyer was not a consumer and that his consequential losses were strictly of a commercial nature; hence the exclusion was not "prima facie unconscionable." Nevertheless, the exclusion was unconscionable *in fact*. Because the station operator was an illiterate high school dropout, the oil company had a duty to explain to him the meaning and consequences of the clause which limited his damages. Failure to provide such an explanation served to deprive the buyer of the ability to make an informed choice during the bargaining process.

Moreover, even when the buyer is a literate, informed, and experienced businessman, a remedial limitation can sometimes operate in a way which deprives him of a "fair quantum of remedy." Even though such a buyer has not been deprived of a "meaningful choice" during the bargaining process, the clause can still be invalidated as unconscionable. Such cases usually involve latent defects which were not discoverable until after a contractual limitation period had expired.

EXAMPLE. In *Wilson Trading Corp. v. David Ferguson, Ltd.*, 23 N.Y.2d 398, 297 N.Y.S.2d 108, 244 N.E.2d 685 (1968), buyer, a sweater manufacturer, purchased yarn under a contract which provided that all claims must be made within ten days after receipt of shipment. Buyer claimed that the yarn contained latent defects which could not be discovered within the ten day period. The court indicated, *inter alia*, that if buyer's allegation was true, then the contractual limitation on remedy might be unconscionable. The brief limitation period, coupled with the non-discoverability of the defect, could operate to deprive the buyer of a fair quantum of remedy for breach.

§ 14.4 Remedies for Unconscionability

Once a contract or any clause of a contract is found to be unconscionable, UCC 2–302 specifically authorizes the court to grant one of the following types of relief: (a) The court may refuse to enforce the entire contract; (b) it may strike the unconscionable clause and enforce the remainder of the contract; or (c) it "may so limit the application of any unconscionable clause so as to avoid any unconscionable result." (The "reformation" remedy).

(a) Refusal to Enforce the Entire Agreement

This form of relief is generally granted only when the aggrieved party (usually the buyer) has not yet received any goods or services under the contract. If it is also the case that he has not yet made any payments, then the court, by simply invalidating the entire executory agreement, will automatically restore the parties to their pre-contract positions. If, on the other hand, the buyer has already paid part of the purchase price, judicial invalidation coupled with an order of restitution of those payments will likewise have the effect of restoring the *status quo ante*.

EXAMPLE. In the previously discussed case of *American Home Improvement Inc. v. MacIver*, 105 N.H. 435, 201 A.2d 886 (1964) the parties entered into an agreement for the sale and installation of home siding for a price of $2,568. Before the seller had performed any part of the contract, buyer defaulted. After finding that the goods and services were worth only $959, the court voided the entire contract on grounds of unconscionability. The court noted that because the buyer had "received little or nothing of value," there were no serious obstacles to invalidation *in toto*. In *MacIver* it was not clear whether the buyer had made any payments under the contract. If he had not, then a simple judicial declaration of invalidity would restore the parties to the *status quo ante*. If, on the other hand, buyer had made payments, a declaration of invalidity coupled with an order of restitution, would accomplish the same result.

(b) Striking the Unconscionable Clause Only

When the seller has partially or fully performed the agreement, it is often impossible or infeasible to invalidate the entire agreement. In such cases, the mere excising of a single clause from the contract will often be an adequate remedy for the aggrieved buyer. For example, when the offending clause is one which limits the remedies available to a buyer who has already received and paid for defective goods, a simple expungement of that clause will be an adequate remedy for buyer. After the offending clause is invalidated, the buyer will be able to avail herself of the full range of Article 2 remedies.

(c) Limiting the Application of Any Unconscionable Clause so as to Avoid Any Unconscionable Result (The "Reformation" Remedy)

The third remedial option available under UCC 2–302—"limit[ing] the application of [the] unconscionable clause"—is an extremely radical one in that it permits the court to re-write the contract for the parties, governed only by its own standards of conscionability. While the courts refer to this remedy as a type of "reformation," it is a remedy which bears little resemblance to the type of reformation which is discussed in Chapter 12 supra, i. e. reformation as a remedy for mistakes in integration. When a contract is reformed for a mistake in integration, it is simply "re-written" to conform to the true agreement of the parties. Indeed, in such cases, the courts frequently stress that they are not making a *new* contract for the parties, but are, instead, simply enforcing the agreement which the parties have already made for themselves.

In contrast, when a court "reforms" a contract because of unconscionability, it rewrites the terms of the agreement (often basic terms, such as price) in order to conform *not* to the true agreement of the parties, but instead to the court's own standards of conscionability.

EXAMPLE. In *Jones v. Star Credit Corp.*, 59 Misc.2d 189, 298 N.Y.S.2d 264 (1969), plaintiffs, who were on welfare, contracted to purchase a home freezer for more than $1200. The price included a basic price of $900 and credit charges of over $300. The retail value of the freezer was approximately $300. After the buyers had made a part payment of about $600, they sued to "reform" the agreement. The court found that the contract price was unconscionable; and, reasoning that the Code permits an unconscionable clause to be "limited," the court "reformed" the contract price so that it would equal the amount already paid by plaintiffs—about $600. It must be stressed that reformation was *not* granted for the purpose of conforming the contract to the true agreement of the parties. The written contract *was*, in fact, the parties' true agreement. Instead, "reformation" entailed a re-writing of the price term so that it would conform to the court's own minimum standards of conscionability. This was accomplished "by changing the payments called for therein to equal the amount of payment actually so paid." Other courts, faced with similar facts, have "reformed" the price term so as to conform to the seller's cost plus a "reasonable" profit. The only standards governing such a reformation are the standards imposed by the "chancellor's conscience."

In conclusion, this author believes that reformation as a remedy for unconscionability is a truly radical form of relief. Yet, it appears to have encountered little opposition from either the courts or the commentators. This acquiescence can probably be explained only by examining the procedural context in which the "reformation" remedy has been granted. In all such sales cases encountered by this author, the party aggrieved by the unconscionable clause was not *affirmatively* seeking to recover expectation damages based on the contract as "reformed." Instead, he was simply seeking (and sometimes able to obtain) relief from his contractual duty to pay the entire contract price. It is unlikely that the courts will be amenable to using UCC 2–302's "reformation" remedy as a means of creating unbargained for expectations on the part of the aggrieved party for which he can affirmatively recover expectation damages.

INDEX

References are to Pages

INDEX

[*313*]

INDEX

INDEX

INDEX

INDEX

INDEX

INDEX

†